# AUTOMATIC TRANSMISSIONS

## NATEF Standards Lab Manual—AT 107

Jack Erjavec/Jim Clarke

**Vice President, Technology and Trades SBU:**
Alar Elken

**Editorial Director:**
Sandy Clark

**Senior Acquisitions Editor:**
David Boello

**Development Editor:**
Christopher Shortt

**Marketing Director:**
Dave Garza

**Channel Manager:**
Bill Lawrensen

**Marketing Coordinator:**
Mark Pierro

**Production Director:**
Mary Ellen Black

**Production Manager:**
Larry Main

**Content Consultant:**
James Clarke

**Production Coordinator:**
Dawn Jacobson

**Project Editor:**
Toni Hansen

**Art-Design Specialist:**
Rachel Baker

**Editorial Assistant:**
Kevin Rivenburg

COPYRIGHT © 2005 Thomson Delmar Learning. Thomson, the Star Logo, and Delmar Learning are trademarks used herein under license.

Printed in Canada
6 7 8  08 07 06

For more information contact
Thomson Delmar Learning
Executive Woods
5 Maxwell Drive, PO Box 8007,
Clifton Park, NY 12065-8007
Or find us on the World Wide Web at
www.delmarlearning.com

ALL RIGHTS RESERVED. No part of this work covered by the copyright hereon may be reproduced in any form or by any means—graphic, electronic, or mechanical, including photocopying, recording, taping, Web distribution, or information storage and retrieval systems—without the written permission of the publisher.

For permission to use material from the text or product, contact us by
Tel.      (800) 730-2214
Fax      (800) 730-2215
www.thomsonrights.com

Library of Congress Cataloging-in-Publication Data:
Card Number:

ISBN: 1-4018-8116-5

## NOTICE TO THE READER

Publisher does not warrant or guarantee any of the products described herein or perform any independent analysis in connection with any of the product information contained herein. Publisher does not assume, and expressly disclaims, any obligation to obtain and include information other than that provided to it by the manufacturer.

The reader is expressly warned to consider and adopt all safety precautions that might be indicated by the activities herein and to avoid all potential hazards. By following the instructions contained herein, the reader willingly assumes all risks in connection with such instructions.

The publisher makes no representation or warranties of any kind, including but not limited to, the warranties of fitness for particular purpose or merchantability, nor are any such representations implied with respect to the material set forth herein, and the publisher takes no responsibility with respect to such material. The publisher shall not be liable for any special, consequential, or exemplary damages resulting, in whole or part, from the readers' use of, or reliance upon, this material.

# CONTENTS

Introduction Information Sheet ... 1

**CHAPTER 37/38    Automatic Transmissions/Transaxles**
Information Sheet / Overhauling an Automatic Transmission/Transaxle (Ch. 37/38) ... 5
Job Sheet AT 107-1 / Disassemble and Inspect a Transmission (Ch. 37/38) ... 7
Job Sheet AT 107-2 / Servicing a Transmission Oil Pump (Ch. 37/38) ... 11
Job Sheet AT 107-3 / Servicing Oil Delivery Seals (Ch. 37/38) ... 13
Job Sheet AT 107-4 / Servicing Planetary Gear Assemblies (Ch. 37/38) ... 17
Job Sheet AT 107-5 / Inspecting Thrust Washers, Bushings, and Bearings (Ch. 37/38) ... 21
Job Sheet AT 107-6 / Valve Body Service (Ch. 37/38) ... 25
Job Sheet AT 107-7 / Overhauling a Multiple-Disc Clutch Assembly (Ch. 37/38) ... 29
Job Sheet AT 107-8 / Inspecting Supply Devices (Ch. 37/38) ... 33
Job Sheet AT 107-9 / Servo and Accumulator Service (Ch. 37/38) ... 37
Job Sheet AT 107-10 / Servicing Governors (Ch. 37/38) ... 41
Job Sheet AT 107-11 / Servicing the Parking Pawl Assembly (Ch. 37/38) ... 43
Job Sheet AT 107-12 / Transmission Case Service (Ch. 37/38) ... 45
Job Sheet AT 107-13 / Reassembly of a Transmission/Transaxle (Ch. 37/38) ... 49
Job Sheet AT 107-14 / Lock-Up Torque Converter Operation (Ch. 37/38) ... 55
Job Sheet AT 107-15 / Filter and Fluid Change (Ch. 37/38) ... 59
Job Sheet AT 107-16 / Visual Inspection of an Automatic Transmission/Transaxle (Ch. 37/38) ... 63
Job Sheet AT 107-17 / Disassemble and Inspect a Transmission (Ch. 37/38) ... 65
Job Sheet AT 107-18 / Servicing a Transmission Oil Pump (Ch. 37/38) ... 69
Job Sheet AT 107-19 / Servicing Oil Delivery Seals (Ch. 37/38) ... 71
Job Sheet AT 107-20 / Servicing Planetary Gear Assemblies (Ch. 37/38) ... 75
Job Sheet AT 107-21 / Inspecting Thrust Washers, Bushings, and Bearings (Ch. 37/38) ... 79
Job Sheet AT 107-22 / Valve Body Service (Ch. 37/38) ... 83
Job Sheet AT 107-23 / Overhauling a Multiple-Disc Clutch Assembly (Ch. 37/38) ... 87
Job Sheet AT 107-24 / Inspecting Supply Devices (Ch. 37/38) ... 91
Job Sheet AT 107-25 / Servo and Accumulator Service (Ch. 37/38) ... 95
Job Sheet AT 107-26 / Servicing Governors (Ch. 37/38) ... 99
Job Sheet AT 107-27 / Servicing Internal Transaxle Drives (Ch. 37/38) ... 101
Job Sheet AT 107-28 / Servicing Final Drive Components (Ch. 37/38) ... 105
Job Sheet AT 107-29 / Servicing the Parking Pawl Assembly (Ch. 37/38) ... 109
Job Sheet AT 107-30 / Transmission Case Service (Ch. 37/38) ... 111
Job Sheet AT 107-31 / Adjusting an External Band (Ch. 37/38) ... 115
Job Sheet AT 107-32 / Reassembly of a Transmission/Transaxle (Ch. 37/38) ... 117
Job Sheet AT 107-33 / Electronically Controlled Transmission/Transaxle Operation (Ch. 37/38) ... 123
Case Study (Ch. 37/38) ... 127
**Review Questions** (Ch. 37/38) ... 128
ASE Prep Test ... 129

# INFORMATION SHEET

## AUTOMATIC TRANSMISSIONS AND TRANSAXLES

### General Information

Many rear-wheel-drive and four-wheel-drive vehicles are equipped with automatic transmissions. An automatic transmission or transaxle selects gear ratios according to engine speed, power train load, vehicle speed, and other operating factors. Nearly all late-model transmissions are electronically controlled. This simply means the hydraulic circuits inside the transmission are controlled by electronics.

Automatic transmissions use a fluid clutch known as a torque converter to transfer engine torque from the engine to the transmission. A torque converter operates through hydraulic force provided by automatic transmission fluid. The torque converter automatically engages and disengages power from the engine to the transmission in relation to engine revolutions per minute. While the engine is running at the correct idle speed, there is not enough fluid flow to transfer power through the torque converter. As engine speed increases, the added fluid flow creates sufficient force to transmit engine power through the torque converter to the transmission.

Most transmissions and transaxles are fitted with a lock-up torque converter. A lock-up torque converter eliminates the 10% slip that takes place in a non-lockup torque converter. The engagement of the torque converter clutch greatly improves fuel economy and reduces torque converter operational heat and engine speed.

There are many types of lockup torque converters. The lockup piston clutch is the type installed in most automatic transmission vehicles. There are also fully mechanical lockup converters, centrifugal lock-up converters, and converters that use a viscous coupling.

### Planetary Gears

In automatic transmissions, two or more planetary gear sets are connected together to provide the various gear ratios needed to efficiently move the vehicle. There are three common designs of compound gear sets: the Simpson, Ravingeaux, and Tandem gear sets.

The Simpson gear train is an arrangement of two separate planetary gear sets with a common sun gear, two ring gears, and two planetary pinion carriers.

The Ravingeaux gear train uses two sun gears, one small, and one large. They also have two sets of planetary gears, three long pinions and three short pinions. The planetary pinion gears rotate on their own shafts, which are fastened to a common planetary carrier. A single ring gear surrounds the complete assembly.

Some automatic transmissions use two simple planetary units set in series. In this type of arrangement, gears' set members are not shared. Instead, the holding devices are used to lock different members of the planetary units together. Although the gear train is based on two simple planetary gear sets operating in tandem, the combination of the two planetary units function like a compound unit. Although the two tandem units do not share a common member, certain members are locked together or are integral with each other. Some transaxles house a third planetary unit used only as final drive.

Nonplanetary-based transaxles are used in many Honda, Acura, and Saturn vehicles. These transmissions are unique because they use a constant mesh helical and square cut gears like a manual transmission.

Another unconventional transmission design, CVT, is found in Subaru and some late-model Hondas. Basically, a CVT is a transmission with no fixed forward speeds. The gear ratio varies with engine speed and temperature. Instead of relying on planetary or helicoil gear sets to provide drive ratios, a CVT uses several belts and pulleys. One pulley is the driven member, and the other is the drive. Each pulley has a moveable face and a fixed face. When the moveable face moves, the effective diameter of the pulley changes. The change is effective diameter changes the effective pulley gear ratio.

**Planetary Gear Controls**

Certain parts of the planetary gear train must be held while others must be driven to provide the needed torque multiplication and direction for vehicle operation. *Planetary gear controls* is the general term used to describe transmission bands, servos, and clutches. A band is a braking assembly wrapped around the drum and holding it. A servo assembly hydraulically applies the band. Connected to the drum is a member of the planetary gear train. In contrast to a band, which can only hold a planetary gear member, transmission clutches are capable of both holding and driving members.

Both sprag and roller overrunning clutches are used to hold or drive members of the planetary gear set. These clutches operate mechanically. An overrunning clutch allows rotation in only one direction and operates at all times.

A multiple-disc clutch uses a series of friction discs to transmit torque or apply braking force. The discs have internal teeth that are sized and shaped to mesh with splines on the clutch assembly hub. In turn, this hub is connected to a member of the planetary gear set that will receive the desired braking or transfer force when the clutch is applied or released.

Multiple-disc clutches are enclosed in a large drum-shaped housing that can be either a separate casting or part of the existing transmission housing. This drum is housing also holds the other clutch components: cylinder, hub, piston, piston return springs, seals, pressure plate, friction plates, and snap rings.

**Hydraulic System**

In an automatic transmission, ATF performs several jobs. It transmits engine torque, controls valve body operation, and operates planetary controls such as in multiple-disc clutches, band, and servo mechanisms. It also lubricates shaft bushings, thrust washers and bearings, and planetary gear train assemblies. ATF smoothly develops the action between the clutch friction discs and clutch plates, as well as between rotating drums and stationary bands. It acts as a cooling agent and transfers heat at the transmission cooler assembly while trying to operate the automatic transmission within the desired temperature range. Finally, ATF interacts with the existing chemicals found in the automatic transmission and those developed as a result of operating extremes.

An automatic transmission uses ATF fluid pressure to control the action of the planetary gear sets. This fluid pressure is regulated and directed to automatically change gears automatically through the use of various pressure regulator and control valves.

The torque converter shell at engine speed drives the transmission pump. The purpose of the pump is to create fluid flow in the system. Pump pressure is a variable pressure depending on engine speed, from idle to full throttle. The pressure at any point within the transmission is the result of constant fluid flow from the pump through the valves, orifices, pistons, seals, and bushings in the transmission.

Three types of oil pumps are installed in automatic transmissions: gear, vane, and rotor. The gear-type and vane-type pumps are the most commonly used.

The purpose of the valve body is to sense the load on the engine and drive train, as well as the driver's intentions. It is an aluminum or iron casting with many precisely machined holes and passages that accommodate fluid flow to and from various valves. Internally, the valve body and related parts are bolted together, and the bolts are set to specification with a torque wrench. Some valve bodies are bolted directly to the transmission housing so it becomes part of the housing assembly.

## Electronic Controls

In most new vehicles, automatic transmissions and transaxles are electronically controlled. A computer with a programmed logic and response to input sensors and switches regulates shifting and torque converter lockup. The electronic system controls these two operations by means of solenoid operated valves. With electronic control, information about the engine, fuel, ignition, vacuum, and operating temperature is used to ensure that shifting and lockup take place at exactly the right time.

An electronically controlled lock-up torque converter prevents lockup from occurring in engine modes where noise, vibration, or harshness concerns are most evident.

Although electronically controlled transmissions function in the same way as earlier hydraulically based transmissions, a computer determines their shift points. The computer determines the time and condition of gear changes according to the input signals it receives and the shift schedules it has stored in its memory. Shift schedule logic chooses the proper shift schedule for the current operating conditions. It uses the shift schedule to select the appropriate gear, then determines the correct shift schedule or pattern that should be followed.

Hydraulically controlled transmissions relied on signals from a governor and throttle pressure device to force a shift in gears. Electronically controlled transmissions typically do not have governors or throttle pressure devices. Hydraulically controlled transmissions relied on pressure differential at the sides of a shift valve to hold or change a gear. Electronic transmissions still do. However, the pressure differential is caused by the action of the shift solenoids that allow for changes in pressure on the side of a shift valve. A computer controls these shift solenoids. The solenoids do not directly control the transmission's clutches and bands. These are engaged or disengaged in the same way as hydraulically controlled units. The solenoids simply control the fluid pressures in the transmission and do not perform a mechanical function.

## Diagnostics

Because of the many similarities between a transmission and a transaxle, most of the diagnostic and service procedures are similar. Therefore, all references to a transmission assembly apply equally to a transaxle unless otherwise noted. This rule also holds true for the questions on the ASE certification test for automatic transmissions and transaxles.

Because of the complexities involved in the operation of an automatic transmission, diagnostics can be quite complicated. This is especially true if the technician does not have a thorough understanding of the operation of a normally working transmission.

Before beginning to rebuild or repair a transmission, make sure it has a problem and requires repairs. Gathering as much information as you can to describe the problem will help you decide if the problem is a transmission problem.

One or more of the following conditions usally causes automatic transmission problems: poor engine performance, problems in the hydraulic system, mechanical malfunctions, or improper adjustments. Diagnosis of these problems should begin by checking the condition of the fluid and its level, conducting a thorough visual inspection, and checking the various linkage adjustments.

.

# INFORMATION SHEET

## Overhauling an Automatic Transmission/Transaxle

### INFORMATION

The job sheets in this section are designed to guide you through the disassembly, inspection, overhaul, and reassembly of a typical automatic transmission/transaxle. You may not use all of the job sheets contained in this section depending on the type of transmission/transaxle you have been assigned to work on.

Safety is of the utmost importance when working with automatic transmissions/transaxles. The units are very heavy and can be cumbersome to move. Always get the help of your lab partner or instructor when moving these units on or off of the repair stations. Always wear eye protection when working on the internal parts of the automatic transmission/transaxle, since there are many parts inside the transmission under spring pressure which could cause serious injury to you or those around you. Be sure to consult the assigned service information or your instructor before attempting to disassemble the various subassemblies within the automatic transmission/transaxle.

# ☐ JOB SHEET / AT 107-3

## Servicing Oil Delivery Seals

Name _____ Station _____ Date _____

### Objective

Upon completion of this job sheet, you will be able to inspect oil delivery seal rings, ring grooves, and sealing surface areas.

Refer to **Chapter 37 and 38** in the AUTOMOTIVE TECHNOLOGY book for additional information.

You must be able to perform these task(s) in order to pass the **ASE** test for: **Automatic Drive Trains and Axles**

These job sheets meet the requirements for **NATEF** task(s): **Automatic Transmissions and Transaxles**

**Tools and Materials:**
AUTOMOTIVE TECHNOLOGY 4e (Thomson, Delmar Learning)
Petroleum jelly      Crocus cloth
Seal driver tools    Feeler gauge set

**NATEF TASKS**
II. Automatic Transmissions and Transaxles
Category: D
Task: 3.3 (P-2)

**Protective Gear:**
Goggles or safety glasses with side shields

**Describe the vehicle being worked on:**
Year _____ Make _____ Model _____
VIN _____ Engine type and size _____
Transmission type and model _____

## PROCEDURE GUIDELINES

**NOTE:** *Some of the steps listed here may not pertain to the automatic transmission/transaxle you have been assigned to work on. Consult the service manual and/or the notes/directions given to you by your instructor.*

- Three types of seals are used in automatic transmissions: O-ring and square-cut (lathe-cut), lip, and sealing rings. These seals are designed to stop fluid from leaking out of the transmission and to stop fluid from moving into another circuit of the hydraulic circuit.

- O-ring and square-cut seals are used to seal non-rotating parts. When installing a new O-ring or square-cut seal, coat the entire surface of the seal with assembly lube or petroleum jelly. Make sure you don't stretch or distort the seal while you work it into its holding groove. After a square-cut seal is installed, double check it to make sure it is not twisted. The flat surface of the seal should be parallel with the bore. If it is not, fluid will easily leak past the seal.

- Lip seals that are used to seal a shaft typically have a metal flange around their outside diameter. The shaft rides on the lip seal at the inside diameter of the seal assembly. The rigid outer diameter provides a mounting point for the lip seal and is pressed into a bore. Once pressed into the bore, the outer diameter of the seal prevents fluid from leaking into the bore, while the inner lip seal prevents leakage past the shaft.

- Piston lip seals are set into a machined groove on the piston. This type of lip seal is not housed in a rigid metal flange. They are designed to be flexible and provide a seal while the piston moves up and down. While the piston moves, the lip flexes up and down. The most important thing to keep in mind while installing a lip seal is: make sure the lip is facing in the correct direction. The lip should always be aimed toward the source of pressurized fluid. If installed backwards, fluid under pressure will easily leak past the seal. Also remember to make sure the surfaces to be sealed are clean and not damaged.

- Teflon or metal sealing rings are commonly used to seal servo pistons, oil pump covers, and shafts. These rings may be designed to provide for a seal, but they may also be designed to allow a controlled amount of fluid leakage. Sealing rings are either solid rings or are cut. Cut sealing rings are one of three designs: open-end, butt-end, or locking-end.

- Solid sealing rings are made of a Teflon-based material and are never reused. To remove them, simply (but carefully) cut the seal after it has been pried out of its groove. Installing a new solid sealing ring requires special tools. These tools allow you to stretch the seal while pushing it into position. Never attempt to install a solid seal without the proper tools. Because these seals are soft, they are easily distorted and damaged.

- Open-end sealing rings fit loosely into a machined groove. The ends of the rings do not touch when they are installed. This type of ring is typically removed and installed with a pair of snap ring pliers. The ring should be expanded just enough to move it off or onto the shaft.

- Butt-end sealing rings are designed so that their ends butt up or touch each other once the seal is in place. This type of seal can be removed with a small screwdriver. The blade of the screwdriver is used to work the ring out of its groove. To install this type of ring, use a pair of snap ring pliers and expand the ring to move it into position.

- Locking-end rings may have hooked ends that connect or have ends that are cut at an angle to hold the ends together. These seals are removed and installed in the same way as butt-end rings. After these rings are installed, make sure the ends are properly positioned and touching.

- All seals should be checked in their own bores prior to installation. They should be slightly smaller or larger (+ or − 3%) than their groove or bore. If a seal is not the proper size, find one that is. Do not assume that because a particular seal came with the overhaul kit it is the correct one.

- Never install a seal when it is dry. The seal should slide into position and allow the part it seals to slide into it. A dry seal is easily damaged during installation.

- Install only genuine seals recommended by the manufacturer of the transmission.

## PROCEDURE

1. Before installing seals, clean the shaft and/or bore area. ☐ Task completed

2. Carefully inspect these areas for damage. File or stone away any burrs or bad nicks and polish the surfaces with a fine crocus cloth, then clean the area to remove the metal particles. Describe your findings.

_____

_____

3. Lubricate the seal, especially any lip seals, to ease installation. ☐ Task completed

4. All metal sealing rings should also be checked for proper fit. Since these rings seal on their outer diameter, the seal should be inserted in its bore and should feel tight there. If the seal has some form of locking ends,

these should be interlocked prior to trying the seal in its bore. Describe your findings.

_____
_____

5. Check the fit of the sealing rings in their shaft groove. Describe your findings.

_____
_____

6. Check the side clearance of the ring, by placing the ring into its groove and measuring the clearance between the ring and the groove with a feeler gauge. Describe your findings.

_____
_____

7. While checking the clearance, look for nicks in the grooves and for evidence of groove taper or stepping. Describe your findings.

_____
_____

8. Use the correct driver when installing a seal and be careful not to damage the seal during installation. ☐ Task completed

## Problems Encountered

_____
_____
_____

## Instructor's Comments

_____
_____
_____

# ☐ JOB SHEET / AT 107-5

## Inspecting Thrust Washers, Bushings, and Bearings

Name _____ Station _____ Date _____

## Objective

Upon completion of this job sheet, you will be able to inspect, measure, and replace thrust washers and bearings and inspect the bushings in a transmission/transaxle.

Refer to **Chapters 37 and 38** in the AUTOMOTIVE TECHNOLOGY book for additional information.

You must be able to perform these task(s) in order to pass the **ASE** test for: **Automatic Drive Trains and Axles**

These job sheets meet the requirements for **NATEF** task(s): **Automatic Transmissions and Transaxles**

**Tools and Materials:**
AUTOMOTIVE TECHNOLOGY 4e (Thomson, Delmar Learning)
Wire-type feeler gauge set
Bushing puller tool
Bushing driver set

NATEF TASKS
II. Automatic Transmissions and Transaxles
Category: D
Task: 3.2 (P-2)
Task: 3.6 (P-2)

**Protective Gear:**
Goggles or safety glasses with side shields

**Describe the vehicle being worked on:**

Year _____ Make _____ Model _____

VIN _____ Engine type and size _____

## PROCEDURE

**NOTE:** *Some of the steps listed here may not pertain to the automatic transmission/transaxle you have been assigned to work on. Consult the service manual and/or the notes/directions given to you by your instructor.*

1. The best time to inspect thrust washers, bearings, and bushings is during disassembly. The bushings should be inspected for pitting and scoring. Describe their condition.

   _____

   _____

2. Check the depth to which the bushings are installed and the direction of the oil groove, if so equipped, before you remove them. Many bushings that are used in the planetary gearing and output shaft areas have oiling holes in them. Be sure to line the oiling holes up correctly during installation or you may block off oil delivery and destroy the gear train. Describe their condition.

   _____

   _____

3. Observe the lateral movement of the shaft that fits into the bushing. Any noticeable lateral movement indicates wear and the bushing should be replaced. Describe your findings.

_____

_____

4. The amount of clearance between the shaft and the bushing can be checked with a wire-type feeler gauge. Insert the wire between the shaft and the bushing. If the gap is greater than the maximum allowable, the bushing should be replaced. What are the specifications for this gap and how do they compare to your measurement?

_____

_____

5. Measure the inside diameter of the bushing and the outside diameter of the shaft with a vernier type caliper or micrometer. Compare the two and state your conclusions.

_____

_____

6. Most bushings are press-fit into a bore. To remove them they are driven out of the bore with a properly sized bushing tool. Some bushings can be removed with a slide hammer fitted with an expanding or threaded fixture that grips to the inside of the bushing. Another way to remove bushings is to carefully cut one side of the bushing and collapse it. Once collapsed, the bushing can be easily removed with a pair of pliers. What did you use to remove the bushing?

_____

_____

7. Small-bore bushings located in areas where it is difficult to use a bushing tool can be removed by tapping the inside bore of the bushing with threads that match a bolt that fits into the bushing. After the bushing has been tapped, insert the bolt and use a slide hammer to pull the bolt and bushing out of its bore. ☐ Task completed

8. All new bushings should be pre-lubed during transmission assembly and installed with the proper bushing driver. Make sure they are not damaged and are fully seated in their bore. ☐ Task completed

9. The purpose of a thrust washer is to support a thrust load and keep parts from rubbing together. Selective thrust washers come in various thicknesses to take up clearances and adjust shaft endplay. Flat thrust washers and bearings should be inspected for scoring, flaking, and wear that goes through to the base material. Describe their condition.

_____

_____

10. Flat thrust washers should also be checked for broken or weak tabs. These tabs are critical for holding the washer in place. On metal type flat thrust washers, the tabs may appear cracked at the bend of the tab; however, this is a normal appearance. Describe their condition.

_____

_____

11. Only damaged plastic thrust washers will show wear. The only way to check their wear is to measure the thickness and compare it to a new part. Describe their condition.

_____

_____

12. Proper thrust washer thicknesses are important to the operation of an automatic transmission. Always follow the recommended procedure for selecting the proper thrust plate. Use a petroleum jelly type lubricant to hold thrust washers in place during assembly. ☐ Task completed

    **CAUTION:** *Never use white lube or chassis lube. These greases will not mix with the fluid and can plug up orifices, passages, and hold check balls off their seats.*

13. All bearings should be checked for roughness before and after cleaning. ☐ Task completed

14. Carefully examine the inner and outer races, and the rollers, needles, or balls for cracks, pitting, etching, or signs of overheating. Describe their condition.

_____

_____

15. Give a summary of your inspection.

_____

_____

_____

## Problems Encountered

_____

_____

## Instructor's Comments

_____

_____

# ☐ JOB SHEET / AT 107-6

## Valve Body Service

Name _____ Station _____ Date _____

### Objective

Upon completion of this job sheet, you will have the ability to clean, inspect, and disassemble a valve body. This service is usually part of a transmission overhaul, and proficiency in this area is necessary in order to pass the **ASE** test for: **Automatic Transmission and Transaxles.**

Refer to **Chapters 37 and 38** in the AUTOMOTIVE TECHNOLOGY book for additional information.

You must be able to perform these tasks in order to pass the **ASE** test for: **Automatic Transmissions and Transaxles**

These job sheets meet the requirements for **NATEF** task(s): **Automatic Transmissions and Transaxles**

### Tools and Materials:

AUTOMOTIVE TECHNOLOGY 4e (Thomson, Delmar Learning)

Instructor notes
Service manual
All-Data®
Transmission stand or holding fixture
Compressed air source
Lint-free shop towel
Inch-pound torque wrench
OSHA-approved blow gun
Clean solvent

**NATEF TASKS**
II. Automatic Transmissions and Transaxles
Category: D
Task: 1.4 (P-2)

### Protective Gear:

Safety glasses or goggles as required

### Describe the vehicle being worked on:

Model and type of transmission: _____

Vehicle transmission is from:

Year _____ Make _____ Model _____

VIN _____ Engine type and size _____

## PROCEDURE

A. Using an instructor-designated transmission, you will use the appropriate service manual information to remove, clean, and inspect the valve body assembly. **DO NOT** disassemble the valve body unless directed to do so by your instructor.

   1. Mount the transmission to a suitable stand or holding fixture.  ☐ Task completed

   2. Remove the oil pan.  ☐ Task completed

   3. Following the service manual directions, remove the valve body attaching screws in the order instructed by the service manual. If the service manual does not give a specific order of attaching screw  ☐ Task completed

removal, start from the outside of the valve body and work towards the center. Note the location and size of the attaching screws; this is important for proper reassembly to prevent damage to the transmission case.

4. Remove the valve body assembly and set aside for cleaning. Have your instructor inspect your work. ☐ Task completed

**Instructor's Signature**

_____

5. Remove the end plate and covers from the assembly. Watch for check balls that may be present. ☐ Task completed

6. In the space below, draw a simple view of your valve body. Note the location of all valves, bolts, check balls (and size), and any springs.

7. Remove all the gaskets from the assembly, and set them off to the side. ☐ Task completed

8. Thoroughly clean the main body and plates of the assembly as directed by your instructor. Allow the unit to air dry or gently blow it dry using compressed air and an OSHA-approved blowgun. ☐ Task completed

9. Inspect the valve body for signs of damage or cracks. Also check the flatness of the mounting surfaces of the valve body and plates. Describe your findings.

_____

_____

10. Have your instructor review your inspection findings to determine if the valve body will need further service. ☐ Task completed

**Instructor's Recommendation**

_____

11. If your instructor determines that no further service to the valve body is needed, install the check balls to their proper locations. ☐ Task completed

12. Replace the end plates or covers. Install the retaining screws by hand, and then tighten them to the specified torque.

    Record the torque spec used. _____

    If you are ready to reassemble your transmission, you may proceed with the following steps. Otherwise, hold off and complete the rest of this job sheet as directed by your instructor.

13. Install the valve body gaskets in their proper location(s). ☐ Task completed

14. Align the spring-loaded check balls and all other parts as needed. ☐ Task completed

15. Place the gasket on the top of the transfer plate. Align the holes with the transfer plate and the bores in the valve body. ☐ Task completed

16. Position the valve body on the transmission. Align the parking pawl and other internal linkages. Then install the remaining screws by hand. ☐ Task completed

17. Tighten the screws in the specified order to the specified torque. If no specific order was given for tightening the valve body screws, start from the center and work your way outward.

    Record the torque spec used. _____

18. Have your instructor inspect your work.

## Instructor's Signature

_____

## Problems Encountered

_____
_____
_____

## Instructor's Comments

_____
_____
_____

**Automatic Transmissions/Transaxles** 33

# ☐ JOB SHEET / AT 107-8

## Inspecting Supply Devices

Name _____ Station _____ Date _____

## Objective

Upon completion of this job sheet, you will be able to inspect various supply devices of a transmission. Refer to **Chapters 37 and 38** in the AUTOMOTIVE TECHNOLOGY book for additional information.

You must be able to perform these task(s) in order to pass the **ASE** test for: **Automatic Drive Trains and Axles**

These job sheets meet the requirements for **NATEF** task(s): **Automatic Transmissions and Transaxles**

**Tools and Materials:**
AUTOMOTIVE TECHNOLOGY 4e (Thomson, Delmar Learning)
Compressed air and air nozzle    Lint-free shop towels
Supply of clean solvent           Service manual

**Protective Gear:**
Goggles or safety glasses with side shields

NATEF TASKS
II. Automatic Transmissions and Transaxles
Category: D
Task: 4.1 (P-2)
Task: 4.2 (P-1)
Task: 4.3 (P-1)
Task: 4.4 (P-1)
Task: 4.5 (P-2)

**Describe the vehicle being worked on:**

Year _____ Make _____ Model _____

VIN _____ Engine type and size _____

Model and type of transmission _____

# PROCEDURE

**NOTE:** *Some of the steps listed here may not pertain to the automatic transmission/transaxle you have been assigned to work on. Consult the service manual and/or the notes/directions given to you by your instructor.*

1. Disassemble the transmission into major units. Set each unit aside until this job sheet refers to it. Describe any problems you encountered while disassembling the transmission. Be sure to follow the procedures given in the appropriate service manual while taking the transmission apart.

   _____
   _____
   _____
   _____

2. Clean each overrunning clutch assembly in fresh solvent. Allow them to air dry.    ☐ Task completed

**34** Automatic Transmissions/Transaxles

3. Check the rollers and sprags for signs of wear or damage. Describe your findings.
   _____
   _____

4. Check the springs for distortion, distress, and damage. Describe your findings.
   _____
   _____

5. Check the inner race and the cam surfaces for scoring and other damage. Describe your findings.
   _____
   _____

6. Check the condition of the snap rings. Describe your findings.
   _____
   _____

7. Summarize the condition of the overrunning clutch units.
   _____
   _____
   _____
   _____

8. Wipe the transmission's bands clean with a dry, lint-free cloth. ☐ Task completed

9. Check the bands for damage, wear, distortion, and lining faults. Describe your findings.
   _____
   _____

10. Inspect the band apply struts for damage, distortion, and other damage. Describe your findings.
    _____
    _____

11. Summarize the conditions of the bands.
    _____
    _____
    _____
    _____

12. Clean servo and accumulator parts in fresh solvent and allow them to air dry.  ☐ Task completed

13. Inspect their bores for scoring and other damage. Describe their condition.

    _____
    _____

14. Check the piston and piston rod for wear, nicks, burrs, and scoring. Describe your findings.

    _____
    _____

15. Inspect all springs for damage and distortion. Describe their condition.

    _____
    _____

16. Check the mating surfaces between the piston and the walls of their bores for scoring, wear, nicks, and other damage. Describe your findings.

    _____
    _____

17. Check the movement of each piston in its bore. Describe that movement.

    _____
    _____

18. Check the fluid passages for restrictions and clean out any dirt present in the passages. Describe your findings.

    _____
    _____

19. Summarize the condition of the servos and accumulators in this transmission.

    _____
    _____

## Problems Encountered

_____
_____
_____

## Instructor's Comments

_____
_____
_____

# ☐ JOB SHEET / AT 107-9

## Servo and Accumulator Service

Name _____ Station _____ Date _____

## Objective

Upon completion of this job sheet, you will be able to inspect the servo's and accumulator's bore, piston, seals, pin, spring, and retainers.

Refer to **Chapters 37 and 38** in the AUTOMOTIVE TECHNOLOGY book for additional information.

You must be able to perform these task(s) in order to pass the **ASE** test for: **Manual Drive Trains and Axles**

These job sheets meet the requirements for **NATEF** task(s): **Automatic Transmissions and Transaxles**

### Tools and Materials:
AUTOMOTIVE TECHNOLOGY 4e (Thomson, Delmar Learning)
Snap ring pliers     Small file
Crocus cloth         Knife

**NATEF TASKS**
II. Automatic Transmissions and Transaxles
Category: D
Task: 1.5 (P-3)
Task: 1.6 (P-3)

### Protective Gear:
Goggles or safety glasses with side shields

### Describe the vehicle being worked on:
Year _____ Make _____ Model _____
VIN _____ Engine type and size _____
Transmission type and model _____

## PROCEDURE

**NOTE:** *Some of the steps listed here may not pertain to the automatic transmission/transaxle you have been assigned to work on. Consult the service manual and/or the notes/directions given to you by your instructor.*

1. On some transmissions, the servo and accumulator assemblies are serviceable with the transmission in the vehicle. Others require the complete disassembly of the transmission. Before disassembling a servo or any other component, carefully inspect the area to determine the exact cause of the leakage. Do this before cleaning the area around the seal. Look at the path of the fluid leakage and identify other possible sources. These sources could be worn gaskets, loose bolts, cracked housings, or loose line connections. Describe your findings.

   _____

   _____

2. Inspect the outside area of the seal. If it is wet, determine if the oil is leaking out or if it is merely a lubricating film of oil. Describe your findings.

   _____

   _____

**38** Overhauling an Automatic Transmission/Transaxle

3. When removing the servo, continue to look for causes of the leak. Check both the inner and outer parts of the seal for wet oil, which means leakage. Describe your findings.

_____
_____

4. When removing the seal, inspect the sealing surface, or lips. Look for unusual wear, warping, cuts and gouges, or particles embedded in the seal. Describe your findings.

_____
_____

5. Remove the retaining rings and pull the assembly from the bore for cleaning. ☐ Task completed

6. Check the condition of the piston and springs. Cast iron seal rings may not need replacement but rubber and elastomer seals should always be replaced. Describe your findings.

_____
_____

7. Begin the disassembling of an accumulator by removing the accumulator plate snap ring. ☐ Task completed

8. Remove the accumulator plate, the spring and accumulator pistons. If rubber seal rings are installed on the piston, replace them whenever you are servicing the accumulator. ☐ Task completed

9. Lubricate the new accumulator piston ring and carefully install it on the piston. ☐ Task completed

10. Lubricate the accumulator cylinder walls and install the accumulator piston and spring. ☐ Task completed

11. Install the accumulator plate and retaining snap ring. ☐ Task completed

12. A servo is serviced in a similar fashion. The servo's piston, spring, piston rod, and guide should be cleaned and dried. ☐ Task completed

13. Check the servo piston for cracks, burrs, scores, and wear. Servo pistons should be carefully checked for cracks and their fit on the guide pins. Describe your findings.

_____
_____

14. Check the seal groove for defects or damage. Describe your findings.

_____
_____

15. Check cast-iron seal rings to make sure they are able to turn freely in the piston groove. These seal rings are not typically replaced unless they are damaged, so carefully inspect them. Describe your findings.

   _____

   _____

16. Inspect the servo or accumulator spring for possible cracks. Also check where the spring rests against the case or piston. Describe your findings.

   _____

   _____

17. Inspect the servo cylinder for scores or other damage. Describe your findings.

   _____

   _____

18. Move the piston rod through the piston rod guide and check for freedom of movement. Describe your findings.

   _____

   _____

19. Check the band servo components for wear and scoring. Describe your findings.

   _____

   _____

20. When reassembling the servo, lubricate the seal ring with ATF and carefully install it on the piston rod. ☐ Task completed

21. Lubricate and install the piston rod guide with its snap ring into the servo piston. ☐ Task completed

22. Install the servo piston assembly, return spring, and piston guide into the servo cylinder. ☐ Task completed

23. Lubricate and install the new lip seal. ☐ Task completed

## Problems Encountered

_____

_____

_____

## Instructor's Comments

_____

_____

# ☐ JOB SHEET / AT 107-10

## Servicing Governors

Name _____ Station _____ Date _____

## Objective

Upon completion of this job sheet, you will be able to inspect, repair, and replace a governor assembly.

Refer to **Chapters 37 and 38** in the AUTOMOTIVE TECHNOLOGY book for additional information.

You must be able to perform these task(s) in order to pass the **ASE** test for: **Automatic Drive Trains and Axles**

These job sheets meet the requirements for **NATEF** task(s): **Automatic Transmissions and Transaxles**

### Tools and Materials:
AUTOMOTIVE TECHNOLOGY 4e (Thomson, Delmar Learning)
Torque wrench

**NATEF TASKS**
II. Automatic Transmissions and Transaxles
Category: C
Task: 2 (P-3)

### Protective Gear:
Goggles or safety glasses with side shields

### Describe the vehicle being worked on:
Year _____ Make _____ Model _____
VIN _____ Engine type and size _____
Transmission type and model _____

## PROCEDURE

**NOTE:** *Some of the steps listed here may not pertain to the automatic transmission/transaxle you have been assigned to work on. Consult the service manual and/or the notes/directions given to you by your instructor.*

1. If the pressure tests suggest that there is a governor problem, it should be removed, disassembled, cleaned, and inspected. Some governors are mounted internally and the transmission must be removed to service the governor. Others can be serviced by removing the extension housing or oil pan, or by detaching an external retaining clamp and then removing the unit. How did you remove yours?

   _____
   _____
   _____

2. To disassemble a typical governor, remove the primary governor valve from its bore in the governor housing.  ☐ Task completed

3. Remove the secondary valve retaining pin, secondary valve spring, and valve.  ☐ Task completed

4. Thoroughly clean and dry these parts. ☐ Task completed

5. Test each valve in its bore in the governor housing; they should move freely in their bores without sticking or binding. Record your findings.

_____

_____

6. Check the valves for any signs of burning or scoring and replace them if necessary. Record your findings.

_____

_____

7. Inspect the springs for a loss of tension and burning marks and replace if necessary. Record your findings.

_____

_____

8. To reassemble the governor, place the spring around the secondary valve and insert them into the secondary valve bore. ☐ Task completed

9. Insert the retaining pin into the governor housing pin holes. ☐ Task completed

10. Install the primary valve into the governor housing. ☐ Task completed

11. If the governor assembly was removed from the governor support and parking gear, be sure to tighten the bolts to specifications with a torque wrench. After assembly, install the governor and torque the bolts to specifications. What are the specifications?

_____

## Problems Encountered

_____

_____

_____

## Instructor's Comments

_____

_____

_____

# ☐ JOB SHEET / AT 107-11

## Servicing the Parking Pawl Assembly

Name _____ Station _____ Date _____

### Objective

Upon completion of this job sheet, you will be able to inspect and reinstall the parking pawl, shaft, spring, and retainer.

Refer to **Chapters 37 and 38** in the AUTOMOTIVE TECHNOLOGY book for additional information.

You must be able to perform these task(s) in order to pass the **ASE** test for: **Automatic Drive Trains and Axles**

These job sheets meet the requirements for **NATEF** task(s): **Automatic Transmissions and Transaxles**

**Tools and Materials:**
AUTOMOTIVE TECHNOLOGY 4e (Thomson, Delmar Learning)
Basic hand tools

**NATEF TASKS**
II. Automatic Transmissions and Transaxles
Category: D
Task: 9 (P-3)

**Protective Gear:**
Goggles or safety glasses with side shields

**Describe the vehicle being worked on:**
Year _____ Make _____ Model _____
VIN _____ Engine type and size _____

## PROCEDURE

**NOTE:** *Some of the steps listed here may not pertain to the automatic transmission/transaxle you have been assigned to work on. Consult the service manual and/or the notes/directions given to you by your instructor.*

1. The parking pawl assembly is typically not hydraulically activated; instead, the gearshift linkage moves the pawl into position to lock the output shaft of the transmission. The parking pawl can be inspected after the transmission is disassembled or, on some transmissions, while the transmission is still in the vehicle. Are you looking at the parking pawl assembly while the transmission is on a bench or in a vehicle?

   _____

2. Check the pawl assembly for excessive wear and other damage. Describe your findings.

   _____
   _____

3. Check to see how firmly the pawl is in place when the gear selector is shifted into the PARK mode. If the pawl can be easily moved out, it should be repaired or replaced. Describe your findings.

   _____
   _____

4. Examine the engagement lug on the pawl. Make sure it is not rounded off. Describe your findings.
   _____
   _____

5. Most parking pawls pivot on a pin. This also needs to be checked to make sure there is no excessive looseness at this point. Describe your findings.
   _____
   _____

6. The spring that pulls the pawl away from the parking gear must also be checked to make sure it can hold the pawl firmly in place. Describe your findings.
   _____
   _____

7. Check the position and seating of the spring to make sure it will remain in that position during operation. Describe your findings.
   _____
   _____

8. The push rod or operating shaft must provide the correct amount of travel to engage the pawl to the gear. Make sure the shaft is not bent or that the pivot holes in the internal shift linkage are not worn oblong. Describe your findings.
   _____
   _____

## Problems Encountered

_____
_____
_____

## Instructor's Comments

_____
_____
_____

# ☐ JOB SHEET / AT 107-12

## Transmission Case Service

Name _____ Station _____ Date _____

## Objective

Upon completion of this job sheet, you will be able to inspect case bores, passages, vents, bushings, and mating surfaces.

Refer to **Chapters 37 and 38** in the AUTOMOTIVE TECHNOLOGY book for additional information.

You must be able to perform these task(s) in order to pass the **ASE** test for: **Automatic Drive Trains and Axles**

These job sheets meet the requirements for **NATEF** task(s): **Automatic Transmissions and Transaxles**

### Tools and Materials:
AUTOMOTIVE TECHNOLOGY 4e (Thomson, Delmar Learning)
Air nozzle           Straightedge
Crocus cloth         Feeler gauge set

**NATEF TASKS**
II. Automatic Transmissions and Transaxles
Category: D
Task: 1.3 (P-1)
Task: 2.1 (P-2)

### Protective Gear:
Goggles or safety glasses with side shields

### Describe the vehicle being worked on:
Year _____ Make _____ Model _____
VIN _____ Engine type and size _____
Transmission type and model _____

## PROCEDURE

**NOTE:** *Some of the steps listed here may not pertain to the automatic transmission/transaxle you have been assigned to work on. Consult the service manual and/or the notes/directions given to you by your instructor.*

1. The transmission case should be thoroughly cleaned and all passages blown out.   ☐ Task completed

2. The passages can be checked for restrictions by applying compressed air to each one. If air flows from the other end, there is no restriction. Describe your findings.

   _____

   _____

3. To check for leaks, plug off one end of the passage and apply air to the other. If pressure builds up in that passage, there are probably no leaks in it. Describe your findings.

   _____

   _____

## 46  Automatic Transmissions/Transaxles

4. Check the fit of the servo piston in the bore without the seal to be sure it has free travel. There should be no tight spots or binding over the whole range of travel. Any deep scratches or gouges that cause binding of the piston will require case replacement. Describe your findings.

   _____

   _____

5. Accumulator bores are checked the same as servo bores. Describe your findings.

   _____

   _____

6. Check the oil pump bore at the front of the case. Describe your findings.

   _____

   _____

7. Case mounted hydraulic clutch bores are prone to the same problems as servo bores. Look for any scratches or gouges in the sealing area that would affect the rubber seals. It is possible to damage these areas during disassembly, so be careful with tools used during overhaul. Describe your findings.

   _____

   _____

8. Sealing surfaces of the case should be inspected for surface roughness, nicks, or scratches where the seals ride. Imperfections in steel or cast iron parts can usually be polished out with crocus cloth. Describe your findings.

   _____

   _____

9. Check the passages in the case for cross-tracking of one circuit to another. Fill the circuit with solvent and watch to see if the solvent disappears or leaks away. If the solvent goes down, you should check each part of the circuit to find where the leak is. Describe your findings.

   _____

   _____

10. Make sure all necessary check balls were in position during disassembly.  ☐ Task completed

11. Check the valve body mounting area for warpage with a straightedge and feeler gauge. This should be done in several locations. If there is a slight burr or high spot, it can be removed by flat filing the surface. Describe your findings.

    _____

    _____

12. A long straightedge should be laid across the lower flange of the case to check for distortion. Any warpage found here may result in circuit leakage, causing any number of hydraulically related problems. Describe your findings.

   _____

   _____

13. Check all bellhousing bolt holes and dowel pins. Cracks around the bolt holes indicate that the case bolts were tightened with the case out of alignment with the engine block. Describe your findings.

   _____

   _____

14. Check all of the bolts that were removed during disassembly for aluminum on the threads. If so, the thread bore is damaged and should be repaired. Thread repair entails the installation of a thread insert or by retapping the bore. After the threads have been repaired, make sure you thoroughly clean the case. Describe your findings.

   _____

   _____

15. The small screens found during teardown should be inspected for foreign material. Describe your findings.

   _____

   _____

16. Most screens can be removed easily. Care should be taken when cleaning because some cleaning solvents will destroy the plastic screens. Low air pressure (approximately 30 psi) can be used to blow the screens out in a reverse direction. ☐ Task completed

17. Bushings in a transmission case are normally found in the rear of the case and require the same inspection and replacement techniques as other bushings in the transmission. Always be sure that the oil passage to a pressure fed bushing or bearing is open and free of dirt and foreign material. Describe your findings.

   _____

   _____

18. Vents are located in the pump body or transmission case and provide for equalization of pressures in the transmission. These vents can be checked by blowing low pressure air through them, squirting solvent or brake cleaning spray through them, or by pushing a small diameter wire through the vent passage. Describe your findings.

   _____

   _____

**Problems Encountered**
_____
_____
_____

**Instructor's Comments**
_____
_____
_____

**Automatic Transmissions/Transaxles** 49

# ☐ JOB SHEET / AT 107-13

## Reassembly of a Transmission/Transaxle

Name _____ Station _____ Date _____

## Objective

Upon completion of this job sheet, you will be able to properly assemble a transmission or transaxle. Refer to **Chapters 37 and 38** in the AUTOMOTIVE TECHNOLOGY book for additional information. You must be able to perform these task(s) in order to pass the **ASE** test for: **Automatic Drive Trains and Axles** These job sheets meet the requirements for **NATEF** task(s): **Automatic Transmissions and Transaxles**

### Tools and Materials:

AUTOMOTIVE TECHNOLOGY 4e (Thomson, Delmar Learning)

Basic hand tools  Air nozzle

Clean ATF in a tray  Dial indicator

Petroleum jelly

### Protective Gear:

Goggles or safety glasses with side shields

**NATEF TASKS**
II. Automatic Transmissions and Transaxles
Category: D
Task: 1.7 (P-1)
Task: 2.2 (P-2)
Task: 3.7 (p-2)
Task: 3.8 (P-2)
Category: B
Task: 1 (P-1)
Task: 2 (P-1)

### Describe the vehicle being worked on:

Year _____ Make _____ Model _____

VIN _____ Engine type and size _____

Transmission type and model _____

## PROCEDURE

**NOTE:** *Some of the steps listed here may not pertain to the automatic transmission/transaxle you have been assigned to work on. Consult the service manual and/or the notes/directions given to you by your instructor.*

1. Before proceeding with the final assembly of all components, it is important to verify that the case, housing, and parts are clean and free from dust, dirt, and foreign matter.  ☐ Task completed

2. Coat all parts with the proper type of ATF. Soak bands and clutches in the fluid for at least 15 minutes before installing them. All new seals and rings should have been installed before beginning final assembly.  ☐ Task completed

3. Examine all thrust washers carefully and coat them with petroleum jelly before placing them in the housing.  ☐ Task completed

4. Install the thrust ring, piston return spring, thrust washer, and one-way clutch inner race into the case. Align and start the bolts into the inner race from the rear of the case. Torque the bolts to specifications. What are the specifications?

_____

5. Lubricate and install the rear piston into the case. ☐ Task completed

6. After determining the correct number of friction and steel plates, install the steel dished plate first, then the steel and friction plates, and finally the retaining plate and snap ring. How many steels did you have?

   _____

7. Using a suitable blowgun with a rubber tapered tip, air check the rear brake operation. What were the results?

   _____

   _____

8. After the rear brake has been completely assembled, measure the clearance between the snap ring and the retainer plate. Select the proper thickness of retaining plate that will give the correct ring to plate clearance if the measurement does not meet the specified limits. What were the results?

   _____

   _____

9. Slide the governor distributor assembly onto the output shaft from the front of the shaft, install the shaft and governor distributor into the case, using care not to damage the distributor rings. ☐ Task completed

10. On some models, the output shaft, bearing, and appropriate gauging shims are placed into the transmission housing. The output shaft washer and bolt is then installed. While holding the output shaft and gear assembly, torque the output shaft nut to specifications. What are the specifications?

    _____

11. Install a dial indicator and check the travel of the output shaft as it is pushed and pulled. What were the results?

    _____

    _____

12. Remove the gauging shims and install the correct sizes of service shims, output shaft gear, washer, and nut. ☐ Task completed

13. Torque the output shaft nut to specifications. Using an inch-pound torque wrench, check the turning torque of the output shaft and compare this reading to specifications. What were the results?

    _____

    _____

14. Place the small thrust washer on the pilot end of the transaxle output shaft. ☐ Task completed

15. Place the rear clutch assembly, front clutch drum, turbine shaft, and thrust washer into the housing. ☐ Task completed

Automatic Transmissions/Transaxles  51

16. Locate and align the rear clutch over its hub. Gently move the rear clutch and turbine shaft around, rotating the assembly to engage the teeth of the friction discs with the rear clutch hub. Align the direct clutch assembly over the front clutch hub. Move the input shaft back and forth, rotating it so the front clutch friction discs engage with the front clutch hub.  ☐ Task completed

17. Position the thrust washer to the back of the rear planetary carrier.  ☐ Task completed

18. Install the rear planetary carrier and thrust washer into the housing to engage the rear planetary ring gear.  ☐ Task completed

19. Install the front thrust washer and the drive shell assembly, engaging the common sun gear with the planetary pinions in the rear planetary carrier.  ☐ Task completed

20. Assemble the front planetary gear assembly into the front planetary ring gear. Make sure the planetary pinion gear shafts are securely locked to the planetary carrier.  ☐ Task completed

21. Install the one-way sprag into the one-way clutch outer race with the arrow on the sprag facing the front of the transmission.  ☐ Task completed

22. Install the connecting drum with sprag by rotating the drum clockwise using a slight pressure and wobbling to align the plates with the hub and sprag assembly. The connecting drum should now be free to rotate clockwise only. This check will verify that the sprag is correctly installed and operative. What were the results?

_____

_____

23. Install the rear internal gear and the shaft's snap ring.  ☐ Task completed

24. Secure the thrust bearing with petroleum jelly and install the rear planet carrier and the snap ring.  ☐ Task completed

25. Assemble the front and rear clutch drum assemblies together and lay them flat on the bench.  ☐ Task completed

26. Make sure the rear hub thrust bearing is properly seated, then measure from the face of the front clutch drum to the top of the thrust bearing. What did you measure and how does it compare to the specifications?

_____

_____

_____

27. Install the thrust washer and pump front bearing race to the pump.  ☐ Task completed

28. Measure from the pump shaft (bearing race included) to the race of the thrust washer. If the thrust washer is not within the limits, replace it with one of the correct thickness. What were the results?

_____

_____

## 52  Automatic Transmissions/Transaxles

29. Total endplay should now be checked. Set the transmission case on end, front end up. ☐ Task completed

30. Make sure the thrust bearings are secure with petroleum jelly. Pick up the complete front clutch assembly and install it into the case. Be sure all parts are seated before proceeding with the measurement. Using a dial indicator or caliper, measure the distance from the rear hub thrust bearing to the case. What were the results?

    _____

    _____

31. Measure the pump with the front bearing race and gasket installed. The tolerance should fall within specifications. If the difference between the measurements is not within tolerance, select the proper size front bearing race. If it is necessary to change the front bearing race, be sure to change the front clutch thrust washers the same amount. What were the results?

    _____

    _____

32. Install the brake band servo. Use extreme care not to damage the O-rings. Lubricate around the seals. ☐ Task completed

33. Install and torque the retainer bolts to specifications. What are the specifications?

    _____

34. Loosen the piston stem. ☐ Task completed

35. Install the brake band strut and finger tighten the band servo piston stem just enough to keep the band and strut snug or from falling out. Do not adjust the band at this time. ☐ Task completed

36. Air check for proper performance. What were the results?

    _____

    _____

37. Place some petroleum jelly on two or three spots around the oil pump gasket and position it on the transaxle housing. ☐ Task completed

38. Align the pump and install the pump with care. ☐ Task completed

39. Tighten the pump attaching bolts to specifications in the specified order. What are the specifications and the specified order?

    _____

40. Check the rotation of the input shaft. If the shaft does not rotate, disassemble the transmission to locate the misplaced thrust washer. What were the results?

    _____

    _____

41. Install bell housing and torque the retaining bolts to specifications. What are the specifications?

42. Adjust the band, after you check to make sure that the brake band strut is correctly installed. ☐ Task completed

43. Torque the piston stem to specifications. What are the specifications?

44. Back off two (or the number specified by the manufacturer) full turns and secure with locknut. What are the specifications?

45. Tighten the locknut to specifications. What are the specifications?

46. Before proceeding with the installation of the valve body assembly, it is good practice to perform a final air check of all assembled components. This will ensure that you have not overlooked the tightening of any bolts or damaged any seals during assembly. What are the specifications?

47. Assemble the parking pawl assembly. Place the assembly into its position and install the extension housing with a new gasket, then tighten the attaching bolts to the proper specifications. What are the specifications?

48. On transaxles, the differential assembly should be disassembled, cleaned, inspected, and reassembled. After it has been reassembled, measure its endplay with gauging shims. Then select a shim thick enough to correct the endplay. What are the specifications?

49. After installing the proper shims, measure the differential turning torque with an inch-pound torque wrench. What were your results?

50. Install the valve body. Be sure the manual valve is in alignment with the selector pin. Tighten the valve body attaching bolts to the specified torque. What are the specifications?

51. Before installing the vacuum modulator valve, it is good practice to measure the depth of the hole in which it is inserted. This measurement determines the correct rod length to ensure proper performance. Refer to the service manual to determine the correct rod length based on your measurements. ☐ Task completed

52. Before installing the kickdown solenoid or other solenoids, check to verify that they are operating properly. Connect the solenoid to a 12-volt source and ground the other terminal. What happened?

_____

_____

53. Install the kickdown switch. ☐ Task completed

54. Before installing the oil pan, check the alignment and operation of the control lever and parking pawl engagement. Make a final check to be sure all bolts are installed in the valve body. ☐ Task completed

55. Install the oil pan with a new gasket. Torque the bolts to specifications. What are the specifications?

_____

56. Lubricate the oil pump's lip seal and the converter neck before installing the converter. ☐ Task completed

57. Install the converter, making sure that the converter is properly meshed with the oil pump drive gear. ☐ Task completed

58. The transmission is now ready for installation into the vehicle. Use the reverse of the removal procedures. Remember to follow proper fluid filling procedures. ☐ Task completed

## Problems Encountered

_____

_____

_____

## Instructor's Comments

_____

_____

_____

# ☐ JOB SHEET AT / 107-14

## Lock-up Torque Converter Operation

Name _____ Station _____ Date _____

## Objective

Upon completion of this job sheet, you will explain the operation of a lock-up torque converter and be able to identify symptoms of lock-up torque converter clutch malfunctions and possible repair solutions.

Refer to **Chapters 37 and 38** in the AUTOMOTIVE TECHNOLOGY book for additional information.

You must be able to perform these tasks in order to pass the **ASE** test for: **Automatic Transmissions and Transaxles**

These job sheets meet the requirements for **NATEF** task(s): **Automatic Transmissions and Transaxles**

**Tools and Materials:**
AUTOMOTIVE TECHNOLOGY 4e (Thomson, Delmar Learning)
Instructor notes
Service manual
All-Data®

**NATEF TASKS**
II. Automatic Transmissions and Transaxles
Category: A
Task: 4 (P-1)
Task: 7 (P-1)
Task: 8 (P-1)
Task: 9 (P-1)

**Protective Gear:**
N/A

**Describe the vehicle being worked on:**

Year _____ Make _____ Model _____
VIN _____ Engine type and size _____

## PROCEDURE

A. Using an instructor-designated vehicle, the student will check the fluid level and condition and record the findings.

 1. Record the procedures you followed to properly check the transmission fluid level.

 _____
 _____
 _____

 2. Remove the dipstick, and record the fluid level and condition.

  a. Fluid level _____

  b. Fluid condition _____

# 56  Automatic Transmissions/Transaxles

3. What is indicated by the fluid's condition?
   _____
   _____

B. Use the service manual, instructor notes, AUTOMOTIVE TECHNOLOGY book, or All-Data® to answer the following questions about an instructor-designated vehicle.

   1. At what speed(s) should the torque converter clutch engage?
      _____
      _____
      _____
      _____

   2. During what conditions should the torque converter clutch disengage?
      _____
      _____
      _____
      _____

   3. What would happen if the torque converter clutch failed to disengage?
      _____
      _____
      _____
      _____

   4. What would happen if the torque converter failed to engage?
      _____
      _____
      _____
      _____

   5. Find the diagnostic codes that are listed in the service information that pertain to the torque converter clutch and list them below.
      _____
      _____

## Automatic Transmissions/Transaxles 57

**Problems Encountered**

**Instructor's Comments**

# ☐ JOB SHEET / AT 107-15

## Filter and Fluid Change

Name _____  Station _____  Date _____

## Objective

Upon completion of this job sheet, you will be able to replace the fluid and filter in an automatic transmission/transaxle.

Refer to **Chapters 37 and 38** in the AUTOMOTIVE TECHNOLOGY book for additional information.

You must be able to perform these task(s) in order to pass the **ASE** test for: **Automatic Drive Trains and Axles**

These job sheets meet the requirements for **NATEF** task(s): **Automatic Transmissions and Transaxles**

### Tools and Materials:

AUTOMOTIVE TECHNOLOGY 4e (Thomson, Delmar Learning)
Lift
Large drain pan
Lint-free rags
Inch-pound torque wrench

**NATEF TASKS**
II. Automatic Transmissions and Transaxles
Category: B
Task: 2 (P-1)

### Protective Gear:

Goggles or safety glasses with side shields

### Describe the vehicle being worked on:

Year _____ Make _____ Model _____
VIN _____ Engine type and size _____
Transmission type and model _____

## PROCEDURE

**NOTE:** *Some of the steps listed here may not pertain to the automatic transmission/transaxle you have been assigned to work on. Consult the service manual and/or the notes/directions given to you by your instructor.*

1. Properly position the vehicle on a lift.  ☐ Task completed

2. Locate the transmission oil pan. Remove or move any part of the vehicle that may interfere with the removal of the pan. What did you need to move?

   _____
   _____
   _____

3. Position the oil drain pan under the transmission pan.  ☐ Task completed

4. Loosen all of the pan bolts and remove all but three at one end. Why do you do this?

   _____
   _____

5. After most of the fluid has drained from the pan, support the pan with one hand. Now, remove the remaining bolts and pour the rest of the transmission fluid into the drain pan.  ☐ Task completed

6. Carefully inspect the oil pan and the residue in it. Record your findings. What is indicated by the fluid's condition?

_____
_____
_____

7. Remove the old pan gasket and wipe the pan clean with a clean lint-free rag.  ☐ Task completed

8. Unbolt the fluid filter from the transmission's valve body. Keep the drain pan under the transmission while doing this.  ☐ Task completed

9. Gather the new filter and gaskets. Compare the old with the new. What did you find? If there is a difference, what should you do?

_____
_____

10. Install the new filter onto the valve body and tighten the attaching bolts to the proper specifications. What are the specifications?

_____

11. Lay the new pan gasket over the sealing area of the oil pan. Make sure the holes line up properly.  ☐ Task completed

12. Position the pan onto the transmission.  ☐ Task completed

13. Install the attaching bolts and hand-tighten each.  ☐ Task completed

14. Tighten the bolts to the specified torque. Make sure you stagger the tightening. What are the specifications? What order did you follow when tightening the bolts?

_____
_____

15. Lower the vehicle.  ☐ Task completed

16. Pour a little less than the required amount of the recommended fluid into the transmission through the dipstick tube. How much fluid did you put in and what type of fluid was it?

_____

17. Start the engine. Look under the vehicle and check for leaks.  ☐ Task completed

18. With the parking brake applied and the brake pedal depressed, move the gear selector through the gears.  ☐ Task completed

19. After the engine reaches normal operating temperature, place the transmission into PARK. ☐ Task completed

20. Check the fluid level and correct it if necessary. ☐ Task completed

**Problems Encountered**

_____
_____
_____

**Instructor's Comments**

_____
_____
_____

**Automatic Transmissions/Transaxles  63**

## ☐ JOB SHEET / AT 107-16

### Visual Inspection of an Automatic Transmission/Transaxle

Name _____  Station _____  Date _____

### Objective

Upon completion of this job sheet, you will have demonstrated the ability to conduct a preliminary inspection of an automatic transmission or transaxle.

Refer to **Chapters 37 and 38** in the AUTOMOTIVE TECHNOLOGY book for additional information.

You must be able to perform these task(s) in order to pass the **ASE** test for: **Automatic Drive Trains and Axles**

These job sheets meet the requirements for **NATEF** task(s): **Automatic Transmissions and Transaxles**

**Tools and Materials:**
AUTOMOTIVE TECHNOLOGY 4e (Thomson, Delmar Learning)
Service manual
Flashlight

**NATEF TASKS**
II. Automatic Transmissions and Transaxles
Category: A
Task: 1 (P-1)
Task: 4 (P-1)

**Protective Gear:**
Goggles or safety glasses with side shields

**Describe the vehicle being worked on:**

Year _____ Make _____ Model _____

VIN _____ Engine type and size _____

Model and type of transmission:

_____

## PROCEDURE

**NOTE:** *Some of the steps listed here may not pertain to the automatic transmission/transaxle you have been assigned to work on. Consult the service manual and/or the notes/directions given to you by your instructor.*

1. Check the transmission housing for damage, cracks, and signs of leaks. Record your findings and recommendations:

_____

_____

2. Check the slip joint area in the transmission extension housing for leaks. If the transmission is a transaxle, check the area where the inner CV joint is attached to the housing. Record your findings and recommendations:

_____

_____

3. Check for leaks wherever something is attached to the housing. Record your findings and recommendations:
   _____
   _____

4. Check the shift and throttle linkages for looseness, wear, and/or damage. Record your findings and recommendations:
   _____
   _____

5. Check any cables for binding, wear, and/or damage. Record your findings and recommendations:
   _____
   _____

6. Check the condition of all cooler lines and hoses. Record your findings and recommendations:
   _____
   _____

7. Check the condition of the fluid; pay attention to the level, color, smell, and feel of the fluid. Record your findings and recommendations:
   _____
   _____

## Problems Encountered

_____
_____
_____

## Instructor's Comments

_____
_____
_____

Automatic Transmissions/Transaxles 71

# ☐ JOB SHEET / AT 107-19

## Servicing Oil Delivery Seals

Name _____ Station _____ Date _____

## Objective

Upon completion of this job sheet, you will be able to inspect oil delivery seal rings, ring grooves, and sealing surface areas.

Refer to **Chapters 37 and 38** in the AUTOMOTIVE TECHNOLOGY book for additional information.

You must be able to perform these task(s) in order to pass the **ASE** test for: **Automatic Drive Trains and Axles**

These job sheets meet the requirements for **NATEF** task(s): **Automatic Transmissions and Transaxles**

### Tools and Materials:
AUTOMOTIVE TECHNOLOGY 4e (Thomson, Delmar Learning)

Petroleum jelly      Crocus cloth

Seal driver tools    Feeler gauge set

**NATEF TASKS**
II. Automatic Transmissions and Transaxles
Category: D
Task: 3.3 (P-2)

### Protective Gear:
Goggles or safety glasses with side shields

### Describe the vehicle being worked on:

Year _____ Make _____ Model _____

VIN _____ Engine type and size _____

Transmission type and model _____

## PROCEDURE GUIDELINES

**NOTE:** *Some of the steps listed here may not pertain to the automatic transmission/transaxle you have been assigned to work on. Consult the service manual and/or the notes/directions given to you by your instructor.*

- Three types of seals are used in automatic transmissions: O-ring and square-cut (lathe-cut), lip, and sealing rings. These seals are designed to stop fluid from leaking out of the transmission and to stop fluid from moving into another circuit of the hydraulic circuit.

- O-ring and square-cut seals are used to seal non-rotating parts. When installing a new O-ring or square-cut seal, coat the entire surface of the seal with assembly lube or petroleum jelly. Make sure you don't stretch or distort the seal while you work it into its holding groove. After a square-cut seal is installed, double check it to make sure it is not twisted. The flat surface of the seal should be parallel with the bore. If it is not, fluid will easily leak past the seal.

- Lip seals that are used to seal a shaft typically have a metal flange around their outside diameter. The shaft rides on the lip seal at the inside diameter of the seal assembly. The rigid outer diameter provides a mounting point for the lip seal and is pressed into a bore. Once pressed into the bore, the outer diameter of the seal prevents fluid from leaking into the bore, while the inner lip seal prevents leakage past the shaft.

- Piston lip seals are set into a machined groove on the piston. This type of lip seal is not housed in a rigid metal flange. They are designed to be flexible and provide a seal while the piston moves up and down. While the piston moves, the lip flexes up and down. The most important thing to keep in mind while installing a lip seal is: make sure the lip is facing in the correct direction. The lip should always be aimed toward the source of pressurized fluid. If installed backwards, fluid under pressure will easily leak past the seal. Also remember to make sure the surfaces to be sealed are clean and not damaged.

- Teflon or metal sealing rings are commonly used to seal servo pistons, oil pump covers, and shafts. These rings may be designed to provide for a seal, but they may also be designed to allow a controlled amount of fluid leakage. Sealing rings are either solid rings or are cut. Cut sealing rings are one of three designs: open-end, butt-end, or locking-end.

- Solid sealing rings are made of a Teflon-based material and are never reused. To remove them, simply (but carefully) cut the seal after it has been pried out of its groove. Installing a new solid sealing ring requires special tools. These tools allow you to stretch the seal while pushing it into position. Never attempt to install a solid seal without the proper tools. Because these seals are soft, they are easily distorted and damaged.

- Open-end sealing rings fit loosely into a machined groove. The ends of the rings do not touch when they are installed. This type of ring is typically removed and installed with a pair of snap ring pliers. The ring should be expanded just enough to move it off or onto the shaft.

- Butt-end sealing rings are designed so that their ends butt up or touch each other once the seal is in place. This type of seal can be removed with a small screwdriver. The blade of the screwdriver is used to work the ring out of its groove. To install this type of ring, use a pair of snap ring pliers and expand the ring to move it into position.

- Locking-end rings may have hooked ends that connect or have ends that are cut at an angle to hold the ends together. These seals are removed and installed in the same way as butt-end rings. After these rings are installed, make sure the ends are properly positioned and touching.

- All seals should be checked in their own bores prior to installation. They should be slightly smaller or larger (+ or − 3%) than their groove or bore. If a seal is not the proper size, find one that is. Do not assume that because a particular seal came with the overhaul kit it is the correct one.

- Never install a seal when it is dry. The seal should slide into position and allow the part it seals to slide into it. A dry seal is easily damaged during installation.

- Install only genuine seals recommended by the manufacturer of the transmission.

## PROCEDURE

1. Before installing seals, clean the shaft and/or bore area. ☐ Task completed

2. Carefully inspect these areas for damage. File or stone away any burrs or bad nicks and polish the surfaces with a fine crocus cloth, then clean the area to remove the metal particles. Describe your findings.

_____

_____

3. Lubricate the seal, especially any lip seals, to ease installation. ☐ Task completed

4. All metal sealing rings should also be checked for proper fit. Since these rings seal on their outer diameter, the seal should be inserted in its bore

and should feel tight there. If the seal has some form of locking ends, these should be interlocked prior to trying the seal in its bore. Describe your findings.

_____
_____

5. Check the fit of the sealing rings in their shaft groove. Describe your findings.

_____
_____

6. Check the side clearance of the ring, by placing the ring into its groove and measuring the clearance between the ring and the groove with a feeler gauge. Describe your findings.

_____
_____

7. While checking the clearance, look for nicks in the grooves and for evidence of groove taper or stepping. Describe your findings.

_____
_____

8. Use the correct driver when installing a seal and be careful not to damage the seal during installation.  ☐ Task completed

## Problems Encountered

_____
_____
_____

## Instructor's Comments

_____
_____
_____

# JOB SHEET AT / 107-22

## Valve Body Service

Name _____ Station _____ Date _____

## Objective

Upon completion of this job sheet, you will have the ability to clean, inspect, and disassemble a valve body. This service is usually part of a transmission overhaul, and proficiency in this area is necessary in order to pass the **ASE Automatic Transmission and Transaxle Test**.

Refer to **Chapters 37 and 38** in the AUTOMOTIVE TECHNOLOGY book for additional information.

You must be able to perform these tasks in order to pass the **ASE** test for: **Automatic Transmissions and Transaxles**

These job sheets meet the requirements for **NATEF** task(s): **Automatic Transmissions and Transaxles**

### Tools and Materials:

AUTOMOTIVE TECHNOLOGY 4e (Thomson, Delmar Learning)
Instructor notes
Service manual
All-Data®
Transmission stand or holding fixture
Compressed air source
Lint-free shop towels
Inch-pound torque wrench
OSHA-approved blow gun
Clean solvent

**NATEF TASKS**
II. Automatic Transmissions and Transaxles
Category: D
Task: 1.4 (P-2)

### Protective Gear:

Safety glasses or goggles as required

### Describe the vehicle being worked on:

Model and type of transmission: _____

Vehicle transmission is from:

Year _____ Make _____ Model _____

VIN _____ Engine type and size _____

## PROCEDURE

A. Using an instructor-designated transmission, you will use the appropriate service manual information to remove, clean, and inspect the valve body assembly. **DO NOT** disassemble the valve body unless directed to do so by your instructor.

   1. Mount the transmission to a suitable stand or holding fixture.    ☐ Task completed

   2. Remove the oil pan.    ☐ Task completed

3. Following the service manual directions, remove the valve body attaching screws in the order instructed by the service manual. If the service manual does not give a specific order of attaching screw removal, start from the outside of the valve body and work towards the center. Note the location and size of the attaching screws, this is important for proper reassembly to prevent damage to the transmission case. ☐ Task completed

4. Remove the valve body assembly and set aside for cleaning. Have your instructor inspect your work. ☐ Task completed

**Instructor's Signature** _____

5. Remove the end plate and covers from the assembly. Watch for check balls that may be present. ☐ Task completed

6. In the space below, draw a simple view of your valve body. Note the location of all valves, bolts, check balls (and size), and any springs.

7. Remove all the gaskets from the assembly and set them off to the side. ☐ Task completed

8. Thoroughly clean the main body and plates of the assembly as directed by your instructor. Allow the unit to air dry or gently blow it dry using compressed air and an OSHA-approved blowgun. ☐ Task completed

9. Inspect the valve body for signs of damage or cracks. Also check the flatness of the mounting surfaces of the valve body and plates. Describe your findings.

_____

_____

_____

10. Have your instructor review your inspection findings to determine if the valve body will need further service. ☐ Task completed

    Instructor Recommendation _____

11. If your instructor determines that no further service to the valve body is needed, install the check balls to their proper locations. ☐ Task completed

12. Replace the end plates or covers. Install the retaining screws by hand, and then tighten them to the specified torque.

    Record the torque spec used. _____

    If you are ready to reassemble your transmission, you may proceed with the following steps. Otherwise, hold off and complete the rest of this job sheet as directed by your instructor.

13. Install the valve body gaskets in their proper location(s). ☐ Task completed

14. Align the spring-loaded check balls and all other parts as needed. ☐ Task completed

15. Place the gasket on the top of the transfer plate. Align the holes with the transfer plate and the bores in the valve body. ☐ Task completed

16. Position the valve body on the transmission. Align the parking pawl and other internal linkages, then install the remaining screws by hand. ☐ Task completed

17. In the specified order, tighten the screws to the specified torque. If no specific order was given for tightening the valve body screws, start from the center and work your way outward. ☐ Task completed

    Record the torque spec used. _____

18. Have your instructor inspect your work.

## Instructor's Signature

_____

## Problems Encountered

_____
_____
_____

## Instructor's Comments

_____
_____
_____

**Automatic Transmissions/Transaxles** 91

☐ **JOB SHEET / AT 107-24**

## Inspecting Apply Devices

Name _____  Station _____  Date _____

## Objective

Upon completion of this job sheet, you will be able to inspect various apply devices of a transmission. Refer to **Chapters 37 and 38** in the AUTOMOTIVE TECHNOLOGY book for additional information.

You must be able to perform these task(s) in order to pass the **ASE** test for: **Automatic Drive Trains and Axles**

These job sheets meet the requirements for **NATEF** task(s): **Automatic Transmissions and Transaxles**

**Tools and Materials:**

AUTOMOTIVE TECHNOLOGY 4e (Thomson, Delmar Learning)
Compressed air and air nozzle    Lint-free shop towels
Supply of clean solvent          Service manual

**Protective Gear:**
Goggles or safety glasses with side shields

**NATEF TASKS**
II. Automatic Transmissions and Transaxles
Category: D
Task: 4.1 (P-2)
Task: 4.2 (P-1)
Task: 4.3 (P-1)
Task: 4.4 (P-1)
Task: 4.5 (P-1)

**Describe the vehicle being worked on:**

Year _____ Make _____ Model _____

VIN _____ Engine type and size _____

Model and type of transmission _____

## PROCEDURE

**NOTE:** *Some of the steps listed here may not pertain to the automatic transmission/transaxle you have been assigned to work on. Consult the service manual and/or the notes/directions given to you by your instructor.*

1. Disassemble the transmission into major units. Set each unit aside until this job sheet refers to it. Describe any problems you encountered while disassembling the transmission. Be sure to follow the procedures given in the appropriate service manual while taking the transmission apart.

   _____
   _____
   _____
   _____

2. Clean each overrunning clutch assembly in fresh solvent. Allow them to air dry.                                                                  ☐ Task completed

3. Check the rollers and sprags for signs of wear or damage. Describe your findings.

_____

_____

4. Check the springs for distortion, distress, and damage. Describe your findings.

_____

_____

5. Check the inner race and the cam surfaces for scoring and other damage. Describe your findings.

_____

_____

6. Check the condition of the snap rings. Describe your findings.

_____

_____

7. Summarize the condition of the overrunning clutch units.

_____

_____

_____

8. Wipe the transmission's bands clean with a dry, lint-free cloth. ☐ Task completed

9. Check the bands for damage, wear, distortion, and lining faults. Describe your findings.

_____

_____

10. Inspect the band apply struts for damage, distortion, and other damage. Describe your findings.

_____

_____

11. Summarize the conditions of the bands.

_____

_____

_____

12. Clean servo and accumulator parts in fresh solvent and allow them to air dry.   ☐ Task completed

13. Inspect their bores for scoring and other damage. Describe their condition.

    _____
    _____

14. Check the piston and piston rod for wear, nicks, burrs, and scoring. Describe your findings.

    _____
    _____

15. Inspect all springs for damage and distortion. Describe their condition.

    _____
    _____

16. Check the mating surfaces between the piston and the walls of their bores for scoring, wear, nicks, and other damage. Describe your findings.

    _____
    _____

17. Check the movement of each piston in its bore. Describe that movement.

    _____
    _____

18. Check the fluid passages for restrictions and clean out any dirt present in the passages. Describe your findings.

    _____
    _____

19. Summarize the condition of the servos and accumulators in this transmission.

    _____
    _____

## Problems Encountered

_____
_____
_____

## Instructor's Comments

_____
_____
_____

# ☐ JOB SHEET / AT 107-25

## Servo and Accumulator Service

Name _____ Station _____ Date _____

## Objective

Upon completion of this job sheet, you will be able to inspect the servo's and accumulator's bore, piston, seals, pin, spring, and retainers.

Refer to **Chapters 37 and 38** in the AUTOMOTIVE TECHNOLOGY book for additional information.

You must be able to perform these task(s) in order to pass the **ASE** test for: **Automatic Drive Trains and Axles**

These job sheets meet the requirements for **NATEF** task(s): **Automatic Transmissions and Transaxles**

### Tools and Materials:

AUTOMOTIVE TECHNOLOGY 4e (Thomson, Delmar Learning)

Snap ring pliers    Small file

Crocus cloth    Knife

**NATEF TASKS**
II. Automatic Transmissions and Transaxles
Category: D
Task: 1.5 (P-3)
Task: 1.6 (P-3)

### Protective Gear:

Goggles or safety glasses with side shields

### Describe the vehicle being worked on:

Year _____ Make _____ Model _____

VIN _____ Engine type and size _____

Transmission type and model _____

## PROCEDURE

**NOTE:** *Some of the steps listed here may not pertain to the automatic transmission/transaxle you have been assigned to work on. Consult the service manual and/or the notes/directions given to you by your instructor.*

1. On some transmissions, the servo and accumulator assemblies are serviceable with the transmission in the vehicle. Others require the complete disassembly of the transmission. Before disassembling a servo or any other component, carefully inspect the area to determine the exact cause of the leakage. Do this before cleaning the area around the seal. Look at the path of the fluid leakage and identify other possible sources. These sources could be worn gaskets, loose bolts, cracked housings, or loose line connections. Describe your findings.

_____

_____

2. Inspect the outside area of the seal. If it is wet, determine if the oil is leaking out or if it is merely a lubricating film of oil. Describe your findings.

_____

3. When removing the servo, continue to look for causes of the leak. Check both the inner and outer parts of the seal for wet oil, which means leakage. Describe your findings.

_____

_____

4. When removing the seal, inspect the sealing surface, or lips. Look for unusual wear, warping, cuts and gouges, or particles embedded in the seal. Describe your findings.

_____

_____

5. Remove the retaining rings and pull the assembly from the bore for cleaning. ☐ Task completed

6. Check the condition of the piston and springs. Cast iron seal rings may not need replacement but rubber and elastomer seals should always be replaced. Describe your findings.

_____

_____

7. Begin the disassembling of an accumulator by removing the accumulator plate snap ring. ☐ Task completed

8. Remove the accumulator plate, the spring and accumulator pistons. If rubber seal rings are installed on the piston, replace them whenever you are servicing the accumulator. ☐ Task completed

9. Lubricate the new accumulator piston ring and carefully install it on the piston. ☐ Task completed

10. Lubricate the accumulator cylinder walls and install the accumulator piston and spring. ☐ Task completed

11. Install the accumulator plate and retaining snap ring. ☐ Task completed

12. A servo is serviced in a similar fashion. The servo's piston, spring, piston rod, and guide should be cleaned and dried. ☐ Task completed

13. Check the servo piston for cracks, burrs, scores, and wear. Servo pistons should be carefully checked for cracks and their fit on the guide pins. Describe your findings.

_____

_____

14. Check the seal groove for defects or damage. Describe your findings.

_____

_____

15. Check cast-iron seal rings to make sure they are able to turn freely in the piston groove. These seal rings are not typically replaced unless they are damaged, so carefully inspect them. Describe your findings.

   _____
   _____

16. Inspect the servo or accumulator spring for possible cracks. Also check where the spring rests against the case or piston. Describe your findings.

   _____
   _____

17. Inspect the servo cylinder for scores or other damage. Describe your findings.

   _____
   _____

18. Move the piston rod through the piston rod guide and check for freedom of movement. Describe your findings.

   _____
   _____

19. Check the band servo components for wear and scoring. Describe your findings.

   _____
   _____

20. When reassembling the servo, lubricate the seal ring with ATF and carefully install it on the piston rod. ☐ Task completed

21. Lubricate and install the piston rod guide with its snap ring into the servo piston. ☐ Task completed

22. Install the servo piston assembly, return spring, and piston guide into the servo cylinder. ☐ Task completed

23. Lubricate and install the new lip seal. ☐ Task completed

## Problems Encountered

_____
_____
_____

## Instructor's Comments

_____
_____
_____

# ☐ JOB SHEET / AT 107-26

## Servicing Governors

Name _____ Station _____ Date _____

## Objective

Upon completion of this job sheet, you will be able to inspect, repair, and replace a governor assembly.

Refer to **Chapters 37 and 38** in the AUTOMOTIVE TECHNOLOGY book for additional information.

You must be able to perform these task(s) in order to pass the **ASE** test for: **Automatic Drive Trains and Axles**

These job sheets meet the requirements for **NATEF** task(s): **Automatic Transmissions and Transaxles**

### Tools and Materials:
AUTOMOTIVE TECHNOLOGY 4e (Thomson, Delmar Learning)
Torque wrench

**NATEF TASKS**
II. Automatic Transmissions and Transaxles
Category: C
Task: 2 (P-3)

### Protective Gear:
Goggles or safety glasses with side shields

### Describe the vehicle being worked on:

Year _____ Make _____ Model _____

VIN _____ Engine type and size _____

Transmission type and model _____

## PROCEDURE

**NOTE:** *Some of the steps listed here may not pertain to the automatic transmission/transaxle you have been assigned to work on. Consult the service manual and/or the notes/directions given to you by your instructor.*

1. If the pressure tests suggest that there is a governor problem, it should be removed, disassembled, cleaned, and inspected. Some governors are mounted internally and the transmission must be removed to service the governor. Others can be serviced by removing the extension housing or oil pan, or by detaching an external retaining clamp and then removing the unit. How did you remove yours?

   _____

   _____

   _____

2. To disassemble a typical governor, remove the primary governor valve from its bore in the governor housing.   ☐ Task completed

3. Remove the secondary valve retaining pin, secondary valve spring, and valve.   ☐ Task completed

4. Thoroughly clean and dry these parts. ☐ Task completed

5. Test each valve in its bore in the governor housing; they should move freely in their bores without sticking or binding. Record your findings.

_____
_____

6. Check the valves for any signs of burning or scoring and replace them if necessary. Record your findings.

_____
_____

7. Inspect the springs for a loss of tension and burning marks and replace if necessary. Record your findings.

_____
_____

8. To reassemble the governor, place the spring around the secondary valve and insert them into the secondary valve bore. ☐ Task completed

9. Insert the retaining pin into the governor housing pin holes. ☐ Task completed

10. Install the primary valve into the governor housing. ☐ Task completed

11. If the governor assembly was removed from the governor support and parking gear, be sure to tighten the bolts to specifications with a torque wrench. After assembly, install the governor and torque the bolts to specifications. What are the specifications?

_____

## Problems Encountered

_____
_____
_____

## Instructor's Comments

_____
_____
_____

## Problems Encountered

## Instructor's Comments

Automatic Transmissions/Transaxles    109

# ☐ JOB SHEET / AT 107-29

## Servicing the Parking Pawl Assembly

Name _____ Station _____ Date _____

## Objective

Upon completion of this job sheet, you will be able to inspect and reinstall the parking pawl, shaft, spring, and retainer.

Refer to **Chapters 37 and 38** in the AUTOMOTIVE TECHNOLOGY book for additional information.

You must be able to perform these task(s) in order to pass the **ASE** test for: **Automatic Drive Trains and Axles**

These job sheets meet the requirements for **NATEF** task(s): **Automatic Transmissions and Transaxles**

**Tools and Materials:**
AUTOMOTIVE TECHNOLOGY 4e (Thomson, Delmar Learning)
Basic hand tools

**NATEF TASKS**
II. Automatic Transmissions and Transaxles
Category: D
Task: 3.9 (P-3)

**Protective Gear:**
Goggles or safety glasses with side shields

**Describe the vehicle being worked on:**

Year _____ Make _____ Model _____
VIN _____ Engine type and size _____

## PROCEDURE

**NOTE:** *Some of the steps listed here may not pertain to the automatic transmission/transaxle you have been assigned to work on. Consult the service manual and/or the notes/directions given to you by your instructor.*

1. The parking pawl assembly is typically not hydraulically activated; instead, the gearshift linkage moves the pawl into position to lock the output shaft of the transmission. The parking pawl can be inspected after the transmission is disassembled or, on some transmissions, while the transmission is still in the vehicle. Are you looking at the parking pawl assembly while the transmission is on a bench or in a vehicle?

   _____

2. Check the pawl assembly for excessive wear and other damage. Describe your findings.

   _____
   _____

3. Check to see how firmly the pawl is in place when the gear selector is shifted into the PARK mode. If the pawl can be easily moved out, it should be repaired or replaced. Describe your findings.

   _____
   _____

# 110 Automatic Transmissions/Transaxles

4. Examine the engagement lug on the pawl. Make sure it is not rounded off. Describe your findings.
   _____
   _____

5. Most parking pawls pivot on a pin. This also needs to be checked to make sure there is no excessive looseness at this point. Describe your findings.
   _____
   _____

6. The spring that pulls the pawl away from the parking gear must also be checked to make sure it can hold the pawl firmly in place. Describe your findings.
   _____
   _____

7. Check the position and seating of the spring to make sure it will remain in that position during operation. Describe your findings.
   _____
   _____

8. The push rod or operating shaft must provide the correct amount of travel to engage the pawl to the gear. Make sure the shaft is not bent or that the pivot holes in the internal shift linkage are not worn oblong. Describe your findings.
   _____
   _____

## Problems Encountered
_____
_____
_____

## Instructor's Comments
_____
_____
_____

Automatic Transmissions/Transaxles  **111**

☐ **JOB SHEET / AT 107-30**

## Transmission Case Service

Name _____ Station _____ Date _____

### Objective

Upon completion of this job sheet, you will be able to inspect case bores, passages, vents, bushings, and mating surfaces.

Refer to **Chapters 37 and 38** in the AUTOMOTIVE TECHNOLOGY book for additional information.

You must be able to perform these task(s) in order to pass the **ASE** test for: **Automatic Drive Trains and Axles**

These job sheets meet the requirements for **NATEF** task(s): **Automatic Transmissions and Transaxles**

**Tools and Materials:**
AUTOMOTIVE TECHNOLOGY 4e (Thomson, Delmar Learning)
Air nozzle          Straightedge
Crocus cloth        Feeler gauge set

**Protective Gear:**
Goggles or safety glasses with side shields

**NATEF TASKS**
II. Automatic Transmissions and Transaxles
Category: D
Task: 1.3 (P-1)
Task: 1.5 (P-3)
Task: 1.6 (P-3)
Task: 2.6 (P-2)

**Describe the vehicle being worked on:**

Year _____ Make _____ Model _____

VIN _____ Engine type and size _____

Transmission type and model _____

## PROCEDURE

**NOTE:** *Some of the steps listed here may not pertain to the automatic transmission/transaxle you have been assigned to work on. Consult the service manual and/or the notes/directions given to you by your instructor.*

1. The transmission case should be thoroughly cleaned and all passages blown out.   ☐ Task completed

2. The passages can be checked for restrictions by applying compressed air to each one. If air flows from the other end, there is no restriction. Describe your findings.

   _____

   _____

3. To check for leaks, plug off one end of the passage and apply air to the other. If pressure builds up in that passage, there are probably no leaks in it. Describe your findings.

   _____

   _____

4. Check the fit of the servo piston in the bore without the seal to be sure it has free travel. There should be no tight spots or binding over the whole range of travel. Any deep scratches or gouges that cause binding of the piston will require case replacement. Describe your findings.

_____

_____

5. Accumulator bores are checked the same as servo bores. Describe your findings.

_____

_____

6. Check the oil pump bore at the front of the case. Describe your findings.

_____

_____

7. Case mounted hydraulic clutch bores are prone to the same problems as servo bores. Look for any scratches or gouges in the sealing area that would affect the rubber seals. It is possible to damage these areas during disassembly, so be careful with tools used during overhaul. Describe your findings.

_____

_____

8. Sealing surfaces of the case should be inspected for surface roughness, nicks, or scratches where the seals ride. Imperfections in steel or cast iron parts can usually be polished out with crocus cloth. Describe your findings.

_____

_____

9. Check the passages in the case for cross-tracking of one circuit to another. Fill the circuit with solvent and watch to see if the solvent disappears or leaks away. If the solvent goes down, you should check each part of the circuit to find where the leak is. Describe your findings.

_____

_____

10. Make sure all necessary check balls were in position during disassembly.   ☐ Task completed

11. Check the valve body mounting area for warpage with a straightedge and feeler gauge. This should be done in several locations. If there is a slight burr or high spot, it can be removed by flat filing the surface. Describe your findings.

_____

_____

12. A long straightedge should be laid across the lower flange of the case to check for distortion. Any warpage found here may result in circuit leakage, causing any number of hydraulically related problems. Describe your findings.

   _____
   _____

13. Check all bellhousing bolt holes and dowel pins. Cracks around the bolt holes indicate that the case bolts were tightened with the case out of alignment with the engine block. Describe your findings.

   _____
   _____

14. Check all of the bolts that were removed during disassembly for aluminum on the threads. If so, the thread bore is damaged and should be repaired. Thread repair entails the installation of a thread insert or by re-tapping the bore. After the threads have been repaired, make sure you thoroughly clean the case. Describe your findings.

   _____
   _____

15. The small screens found during teardown should be inspected for foreign material. Describe your findings.

   _____
   _____

16. Most screens can be removed easily. Care should be taken when cleaning because some cleaning solvents will destroy the plastic screens. Low air pressure (approximately 30 psi) can be used to blow the screens out in a reverse direction.  ☐ Task completed

17. Bushings in a transmission case are normally found in the rear of the case and require the same inspection and replacement techniques as other bushings in the transmission. Always be sure that the oil passage to a pressure fed bushing or bearing is open and free of dirt and foreign material. Describe your findings.

   _____
   _____

18. Vents are located in the pump body or transmission case and provide for equalization of pressures in the transmission. These vents can be checked by blowing low pressure air through them, squirting solvent or brake cleaning spray through them, or by pushing a small diameter wire through the vent passage. Describe your findings.

   _____
   _____

## Problems Encountered

## Instructor's Comments

# ☐ JOB SHEET / AT 107-31

## Adjusting an External Band

Name _____ Station _____ Date _____

## Objective

Upon completion of this job sheet, you will be able to properly adjust a band with an external adjuster. Refer to **Chapters 37 and 38** in the AUTOMOTIVE TECHNOLOGY book for additional information.

You must be able to perform these task(s) in order to pass the **ASE** test for: **Automatic Drive Trains and Axles**

These job sheets meet the requirements for **NATEF** task(s): **Automatic Transmissions and Transaxles**

**Tools and Materials:**
AUTOMOTIVE TECHNOLOGY 4e (Thomson, Delmar Learning)
Basic hand tools

**NATEF TASKS**
II. Automatic Transmissions and Transaxles
Category: D
Task: 4.5 (P-2)

**Protective Gear:**
Goggles or safety glasses with side shields

**Describe the vehicle being worked on:**

Year _____ Make _____ Model _____

VIN _____ Engine type and size _____

Transmission type and model _____

## PROCEDURE

**NOTE:** *Some of the steps listed here may not pertain to the automatic transmission/transaxle you have been assigned to work on. Consult the service manual and/or the notes/directions given to you by your instructor.*

1. Place the vehicle securely on a lift. ☐ Task completed

2. Locate the transmission identification tag and identify the exact type and model of transmission you are working on. Where was the ID tag?

   _____

   _____

3. Explain how you know the transmission type from the information on the tag.

   _____

   _____

4. Locate the band adjustment screw. Describe its location.

   _____

   _____

## 116 Automatic Transmissions/Transaxles

5. Loosen the adjusting screw locknut. If the locknut has a fluid seal, do not re-use the locknut. Install a new nut. ☐ Task completed

6. Loosen the adjusting screw so that the band can relax around the drum and all tension is off the adjusting screw. ☐ Task completed

7. Tighten the adjusting screw to the specified torque. What is the torque specification?
   _____

8. Back off the adjusting screw the exact number of turns that are specified in the service manual. How many turns did the manual tell you to back off?
   _____

9. Position a wrench on the adjusting screw and over the locknut so that you can tighten the locknut without moving the adjusting screw. ☐ Task completed

10. Hold the adjusting screw in position and tighten the locknut to the specified torque. ☐ Task completed

**Problems Encountered**

_____
_____
_____

**Instructor's Comments**

_____
_____
_____

Automatic Transmissions/Transaxles 117

☐ **JOB SHEET / AT 107-32**

## Reassembly of a Transmission/Transaxle

Name _____ Station _____ Date _____

### Objective

Upon completion of this job sheet, you will be able to properly assemble a transmission or transaxle. Refer to **Chapters 37 and 38** in the AUTOMOTIVE TECHNOLOGY book for additional information. You must be able to perform these task(s) in order to pass the **ASE** test for: **Automatic Drive Trains and Axles** These job sheets meet the requirements for **NATEF** task(s): **Automatic Transmissions and Transaxles**

### Tools and Materials:

AUTOMOTIVE TECHNOLOGY 4e (Thomson, Delmar Learning)

Basic hand tools          Air nozzle
Clean ATF in a tray       Dial indicator
Petroleum jelly

### Protective Gear:

Goggles or safety glasses with side shields

**NATEF TASKS**
II. Automatic Transmissions and Transaxles
Category: B
Task: 1 (P-1)
Task: 2 (P-1)
Category: D
Task: 1.7 (P-1)
Task: 2.2 (P-2)
Task: 3.7 (P-2)
Task: 3.8 (P-2)

### Describe the vehicle being worked on:

Year _____ Make _____ Model _____

VIN _____ Engine type and size _____

Transmission type and model _____

## PROCEDURE

**NOTE:** *Some of the steps listed here may not pertain to the automatic transmission/transaxle you have been assigned to work on. Consult the service manual and/or the notes/directions given to you by your instructor.*

1. Before proceeding with the final assembly of all components, it is important to verify that the case, housing, and parts are clean and free from dust, dirt, and foreign matter.  ☐ Task completed

2. Coat all parts with the proper type of ATF. Soak bands and clutches in the fluid for at least 15 minutes before installing them. All new seals and rings should have been installed before beginning final assembly.  ☐ Task completed

3. Examine all thrust washers carefully and coat them with petroleum jelly before placing them in the housing.  ☐ Task completed

4. Install the thrust ring, piston return spring, thrust washer, and one-way clutch inner race into the case. Align and start the bolts into the inner race from the rear of the case. Torque the bolts to specifications. What are the specifications?

   _____

5. Lubricate and install the rear piston into the case. ☐ Task completed

6. After determining the correct number of friction and steel plates, install the steel dished plate first, then the steel and friction plates, and finally the retaining plate and snap ring. How many steels did you have?

_____

7. Using a suitable blowgun with a rubber tapered tip, air check the rear brake operation. What were the results?

_____

_____

8. After the rear brake has been completely assembled, measure the clearance between the snap ring and the retainer plate. Select the proper thickness of retaining plate that will give the correct ring to plate clearance if the measurement does not meet the specified limits. What were the results?

_____

_____

9. Slide the governor distributor assembly onto the output shaft from the front of the shaft, install the shaft and governor distributor into the case, using care not to damage the distributor rings. ☐ Task completed

10. On some models, the output shaft, bearing, and appropriate gauging shims are placed into the transmission housing. The output shaft washer and bolt is then installed. While holding the output shaft and gear assembly, torque the output shaft nut to specifications. What are the specifications?

_____

11. Install a dial indicator and check the travel of the output shaft as it is pushed and pulled. What were the results?

_____

_____

12. Remove the gauging shims and install the correct sizes of service shims, output shaft gear, washer, and nut. ☐ Task completed

13. Torque the output shaft nut to specifications. Using an inch-pound torque wrench, check the turning torque of the output shaft and compare this reading to specifications. What were the results?

_____

_____

14. Place the small thrust washer on the pilot end of the transaxle output shaft. ☐ Task completed

15. Place the rear clutch assembly, front clutch drum, turbine shaft, and thrust washer into the housing. ☐ Task completed

16. Locate and align the rear clutch over its hub. Gently move the rear clutch and turbine shaft around, rotating the assembly to engage the teeth of the friction discs with the rear clutch hub. Align the direct clutch assembly over the front clutch hub. Move the input shaft back and forth, rotating it so the front clutch friction discs engage with the front clutch hub. ☐ Task completed

17. Position the thrust washer to the back of the rear planetary carrier. ☐ Task completed

18. Install the rear planetary carrier and thrust washer into the housing to engage the rear planetary ring gear. ☐ Task completed

19. Install the front thrust washer and the drive shell assembly, engaging the common sun gear with the planetary pinions in the rear planetary carrier. ☐ Task completed

20. Assemble the front planetary gear assembly into the front planetary ring gear. Make sure the planetary pinion gear shafts are securely locked to the planetary carrier. ☐ Task completed

21. Install the one-way sprag into the one-way clutch outer race with the arrow on the sprag facing the front of the transmission. ☐ Task completed

22. Install the connecting drum with sprag by rotating the drum clockwise using a slight pressure and wobbling to align the plates with the hub and sprag assembly. The connecting drum should now be free to rotate clockwise only. This check will verify that the sprag is correctly installed and operative. What were the results?

   _____

   _____

23. Install the rear internal gear and the shaft's snap ring. ☐ Task completed

24. Secure the thrust bearing with petroleum jelly and install the rear planet carrier and the snap ring. ☐ Task completed

25. Assemble the front and rear clutch drum assemblies together and lay them flat on the bench. ☐ Task completed

26. Make sure the rear hub thrust bearing is properly seated, then measure from the face of the front clutch drum to the top of the thrust bearing. What did you measure and how does it compare to the specifications?

   _____

   _____

   _____

27. Install the thrust washer and pump front bearing race to the pump. ☐ Task completed

28. Measure from the pump shaft (bearing race included) to the race of the thrust washer. If the thrust washer is not within the limits, replace it with one of the correct thickness. What were the results?

   _____

   _____

29. Total endplay should now be checked. Set the transmission case on end, front end up. ☐ Task completed

30. Make sure the thrust bearings are secure with petroleum jelly. Pick up the complete front clutch assembly and install it into the case. Be sure all parts are seated before proceeding with the measurement. Using a dial indicator or caliper, measure the distance from the rear hub thrust bearing to the case. What were the results?

   _____

   _____

31. Measure the pump with the front bearing race and gasket installed. The tolerance should fall within specifications. If the difference between the measurements is not within tolerance, select the proper size front bearing race. If it is necessary to change the front bearing race, be sure to change the front clutch thrust washers the same amount. What were the results?

   _____

   _____

32. Install the brake band servo. Use extreme care not to damage the O-rings. Lubricate around the seals. ☐ Task completed

33. Install and torque the retainer bolts to specifications. What are the specifications?

   _____

34. Loosen the piston stem. ☐ Task completed

35. Install the brake band strut and finger tighten the band servo piston stem just enough to keep the band and strut snug or from falling out. Do not adjust the band at this time. ☐ Task completed

36. Air check for proper performance. What were the results?

   _____

   _____

37. Place some petroleum jelly on two or three spots around the oil pump gasket and position it on the transaxle housing. ☐ Task completed

38. Align the pump and install the pump with care. ☐ Task completed

39. Tighten the pump attaching bolts to specifications in the specified order. What are the specifications and the specified order?

   _____

40. Check the rotation of the input shaft. If the shaft does not rotate, disassemble the transmission to locate the misplaced thrust washer. What were the results?

   _____

   _____

Automatic Transmissions/Transaxles  121

41. Install bell housing and torque the retaining bolts to specifications. What are the specifications?

   _____

42. Adjust the band, after you check to make sure that the brake band strut is correctly installed.  ☐ Task completed

43. Torque the piston stem to specifications. What are the specifications?

   _____

44. Back off two (or the number specified by the manufacturer) full turns and secure with locknut. What are the specifications?

   _____

45. Tighten the locknut to specifications. What are the specifications?

   _____

46. Before proceeding with the installation of the valve body assembly, it is good practice to perform a final air check of all assembled components. This will ensure that you have not overlooked the tightening of any bolts or damaged any seals during assembly. What are the specifications?

   _____

47. Assemble the parking pawl assembly. Place the assembly into its position and install the extension housing with a new gasket, then tighten the attaching bolts to the proper specifications. What are the specifications?

   _____

48. On transaxles, the differential assembly should be disassembled, cleaned, inspected, and reassembled. After it has been reassembled, measure its endplay with gauging shims. Then select a shim thick enough to correct the endplay. What are the specifications?

   _____

49. After installing the proper shims, measure the differential turning torque with an inch-pound torque wrench. What were your results?

   _____

   _____

50. Install the valve body. Be sure the manual valve is in alignment with the selector pin. Tighten the valve body attaching bolts to the specified torque. What are the specifications?

   _____

51. Before installing the vacuum modulator valve, it is good practice to measure the depth of the hole in which it is inserted. This measurement determines the correct rod length to ensure proper performance. Refer to the service manual to determine the correct rod length based on your measurements.  ☐ Task completed

## 122　Automatic Transmissions/Transaxles

52. Before installing the kickdown solenoid or other solenoids, check to verify that they are operating properly. Connect the solenoid to a 12-volt source and ground the other terminal. What happened?

   _____

   _____

53. Install the kickdown switch. ☐ Task completed

54. Before installing the oil pan, check the alignment and operation of the control lever and parking pawl engagement. Make a final check to be sure all bolts are installed in the valve body. ☐ Task completed

55. Install the oil pan with a new gasket. Torque the bolts to specifications. What are the specifications?

   _____

56. Lubricate the oil pump's lip seal and the converter neck before installing the converter. ☐ Task completed

57. Install the converter, making sure that the converter is properly meshed with the oil pump drive gear. ☐ Task completed

58. The transmission is now ready for installation into the vehicle. Use the reverse of the removal procedures. Remember to follow proper fluid filling procedures. ☐ Task completed

## Problems Encountered

_____

_____

_____

## Instructor's Comments

_____

_____

_____

# JOB SHEET / AT 102-33

## Electronically Controlled Transmission Operation

Name _____ Station _____ Date _____

## Objective

Upon completion of this job sheet, you will use the service information available to correctly describe the various solenoids found in an electronically controlled transmission and what their function is.

Refer to **Chapters 37 and 38** in the AUTOMOTIVE TECHNOLOGY book for additional information.

You must be able to perform these tasks in order to pass the **ASE** test for: **Automatic Transmissions and Transaxles**

These job sheets meet the requirements for **NATEF** task(s): **Automatic Transmissions and Transaxles**

**Tools and Materials:**
AUTOMOTIVE TECHNOLOGY 4e (Thomson, Delmar Learning)
Instructor notes
Service manual
All-Data®

**NATEF TASKS**
II. Automatic Transmissions and Transaxles
Category: A
Task: 10 (P-2)

**Protective Gear:**
Safety glasses or goggles as required

## PROCEDURE

On three late-model vehicles with an electronically controlled transmission assigned by your instructor, use the service information available to determine how many solenoids are used in the operation of each transmission. Record what each is doing when the transmission is operating in the various gears.

**Describe the vehicle being worked on:**

Year _____ Make _____ Model _____

VIN _____ Engine type and size _____

1. Number of Solenoids _____

   a. What solenoids are energized in:

   1st gear?

   _____

   _____

   _____

# 124  Automatic Transmissions/Transaxles

2nd gear?

_____

_____

_____

3rd gear?

_____

_____

_____

4th gear?

_____

_____

_____

5th gear?

_____

_____

_____

6th gear?

_____

_____

_____

Reverse gear?

_____

_____

_____

**Describe the vehicle being worked on:**

Year _____ Make _____ Model _____

VIN _____ Engine type and size _____

2. Number of Solenoids _____

   a. What solenoids are energized in:

   1st gear?

   _____

   _____

   _____

2nd gear?
_____
_____
_____

3rd gear?
_____
_____
_____

4th gear?
_____
_____
_____

5th gear?
_____
_____
_____

6th gear?
_____
_____
_____

Reverse gear?
_____
_____
_____

**Describe the vehicle being worked on:**
Year _____ Make _____ Model _____
VIN _____ Engine type and size _____ C.

3. Number of Solenoids _____

   a. What solenoids are energized in:

   1st gear?
   _____
   _____
   _____

2nd gear?

_____
_____

3rd gear?

_____
_____

4th gear?

_____
_____

5th gear?

_____
_____

6th gear?

_____
_____

Reverse gear?

_____
_____

## Problems Encountered

_____
_____

## Instructor's Comments

_____
_____